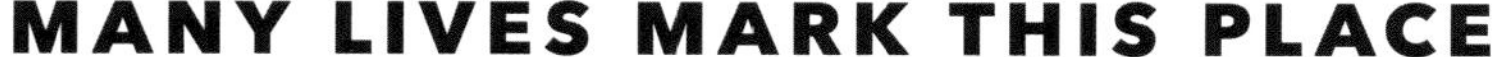

MANY LIVES MARK THIS PLACE

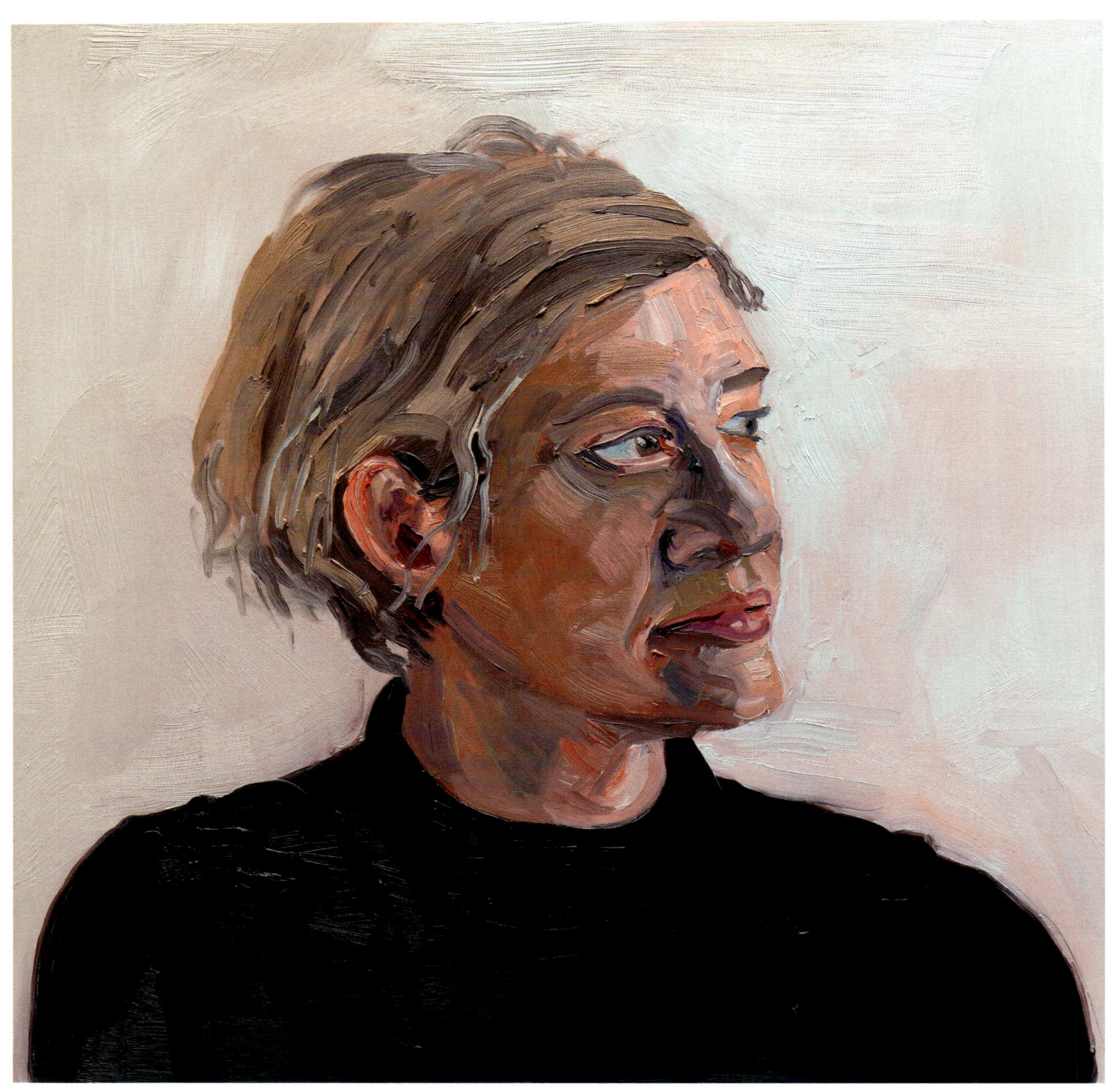

Heather O'Neill 2018
oil on panel
16" × 16"

MANY LIVES MARK THIS PLACE

JOHN HARTMAN

paints Canadian writers in the landscapes that inspire them

FOREWORD BY IAN M. THOM

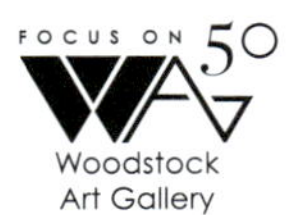

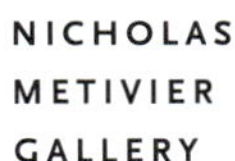

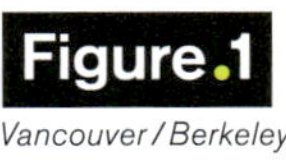

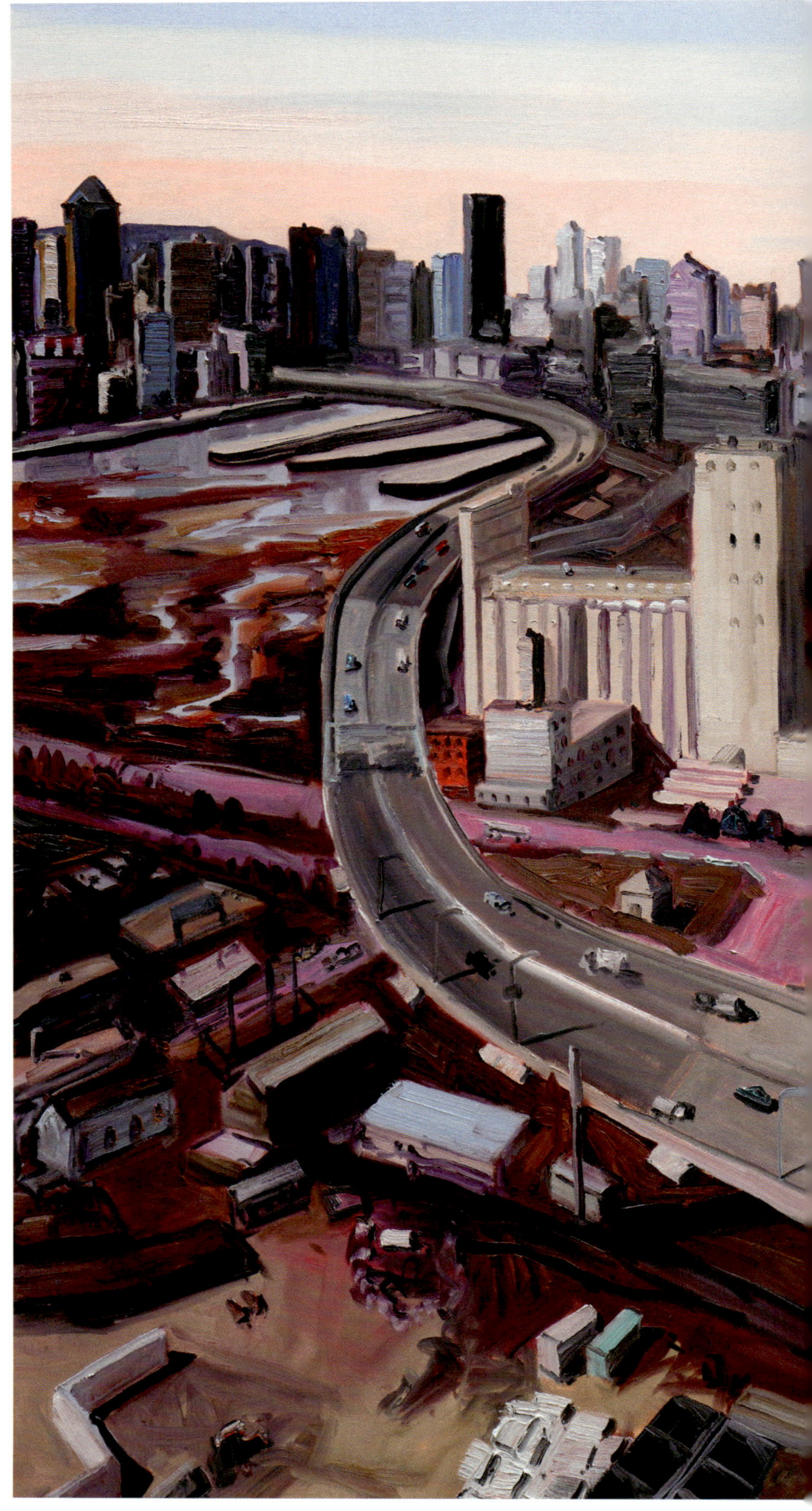

Montreal Harbour 2018
oil on linen
48″ × 68″

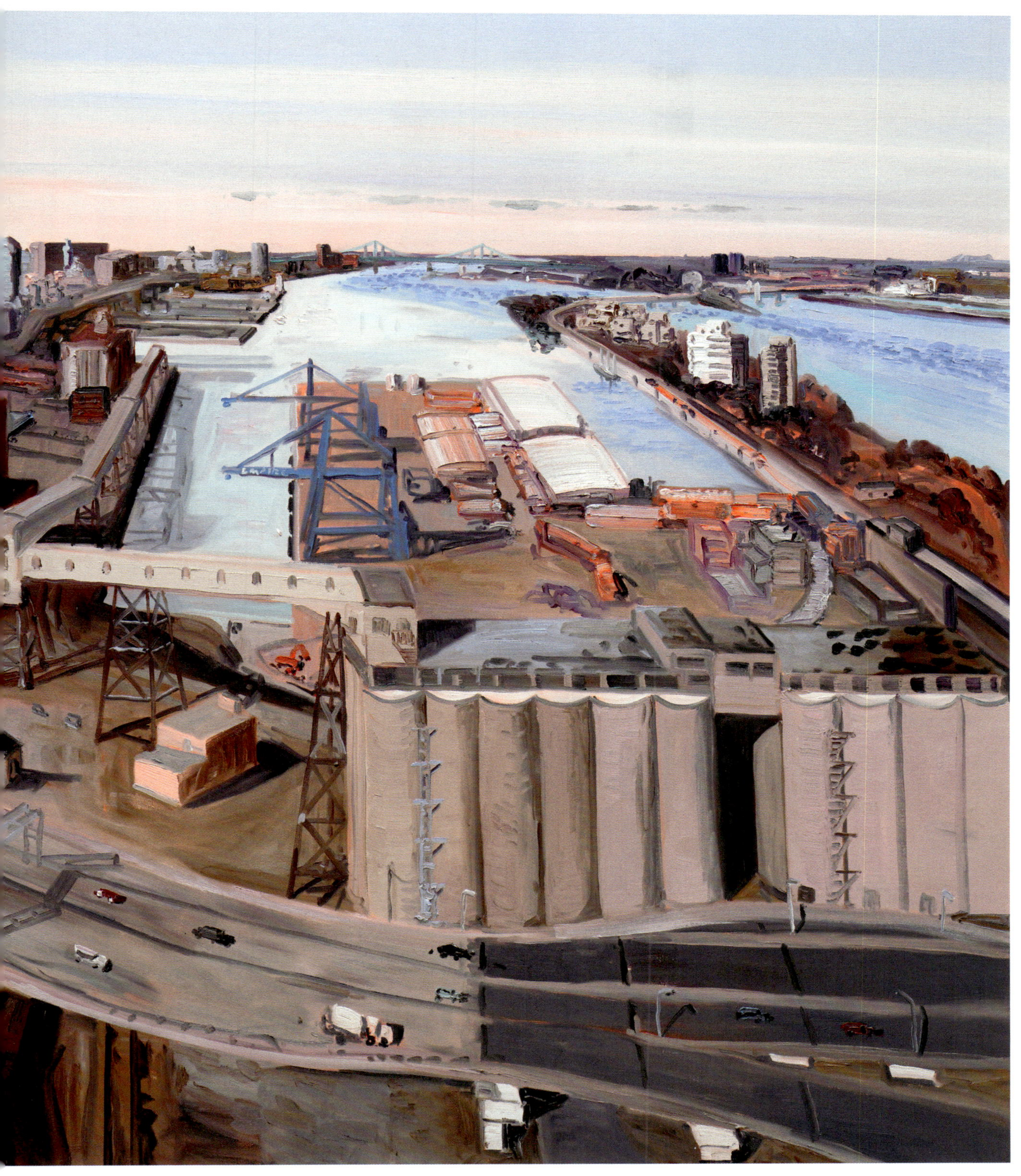

Contents

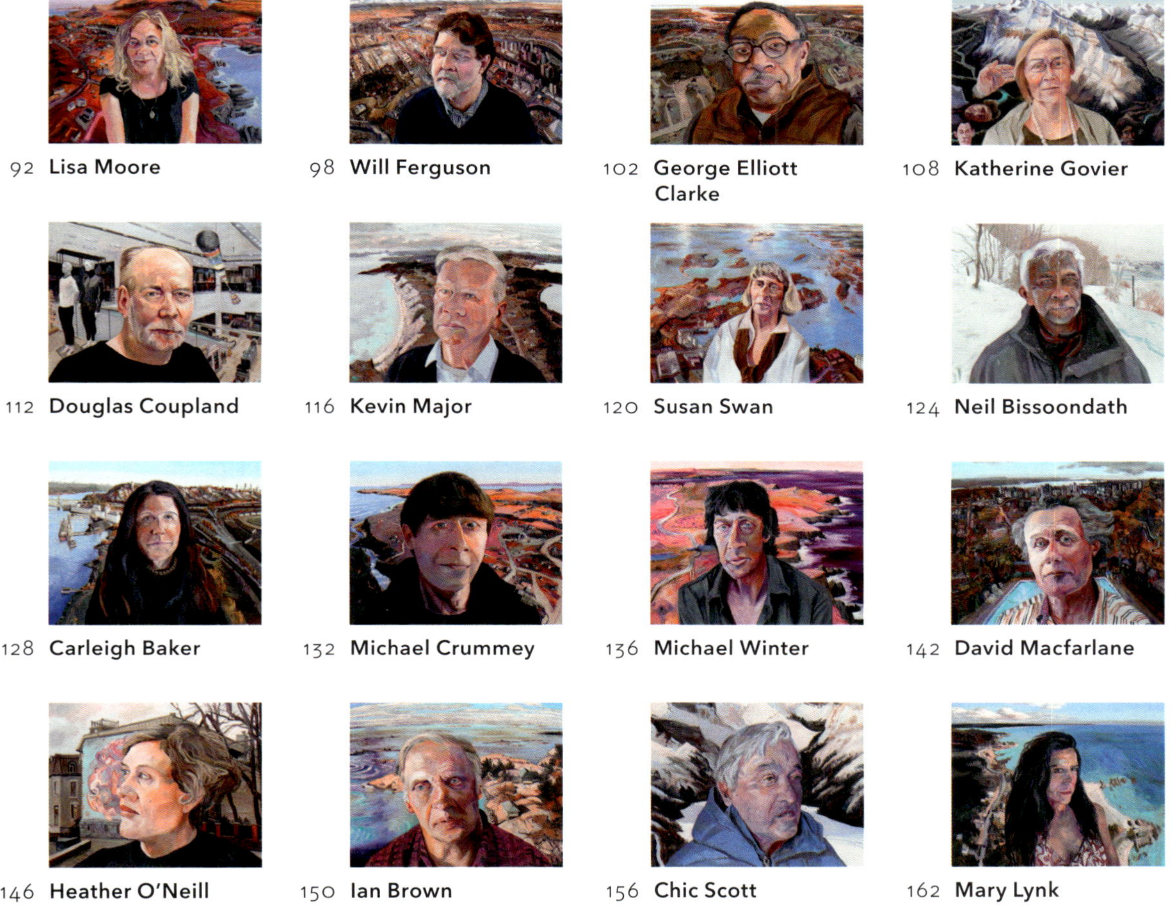

IAN M. THOM

Foreword: John Hartman and the Portrait

JOHN HARTMAN is not an artist who is afraid of challenges, whether as a printmaker who built on the example of David Brown Milne (1882–1953) to explore the exquisitely difficult technique of colour drypoint; as a curator who helped bring the work of the almost forgotten W.J. Wood (1877–1954) back to public consciousness; or as a landscape painter of enormous accomplishment who has sought to reset our understanding of what landscape can be in a country that is, in large measure, defined by its vastness. These have been substantive challenges, and Hartman has moved steadily forward with the conviction that they merit his and our attention. And, I would suggest, he has been proven correct each time. Hartman's prints are now regarded as remarkable images, and W.J. Wood has entered museum and private collections with a place in Canadian art history. Hartman's own landscape work, both paintings and drawings, has been exhibited and collected widely, and he has travelled extensively to depict his chosen subjects. In short, Hartman is not someone who stays in a comfort zone.

I was not aware until recently that Hartman did portraiture, but it turns out that there is a line of portraiture in much of his work. It could be argued that many of his landscapes are portraits of cities and landscapes, from across Canada and around the world. He has also, for the past twenty years, painted friends intermittently. As he puts it,

> My work has centred on trying to create a method that would allow me to paint about the connection between people and place, based on my experiences of both. You can call the more landscape-based work "portraits" without it being wrong, and you could call some of the recent portraits "landscapes with figures." In truth, my painting has always been something of a hybrid that draws on both traditions.

This current project, however, is different in both magnitude and ambition. As the following pages powerfully demonstrate, Hartman has sought to place authors in juxtaposition with landscapes that have particular meanings for them. In many cases, these are not landscapes that Hartman knew, and so they required years of work to capture on canvas. He travelled the breadth of Canada to study these disparate places. So, too, did he travel, meet, and paint the authors. The results are larger than life-sized, and place the subjects not in but against their landscapes—suggesting touchstones of inspiration and ideas for each.

The project began with David Macfarlane, whom Hartman knew because both men have spent time working on Georgian Bay, in Ontario. Macfarlane suggested that he would like to have the landscape element of his portrait set in Hamilton, more specifically against the backyard pool of his parents' house. Together, the two

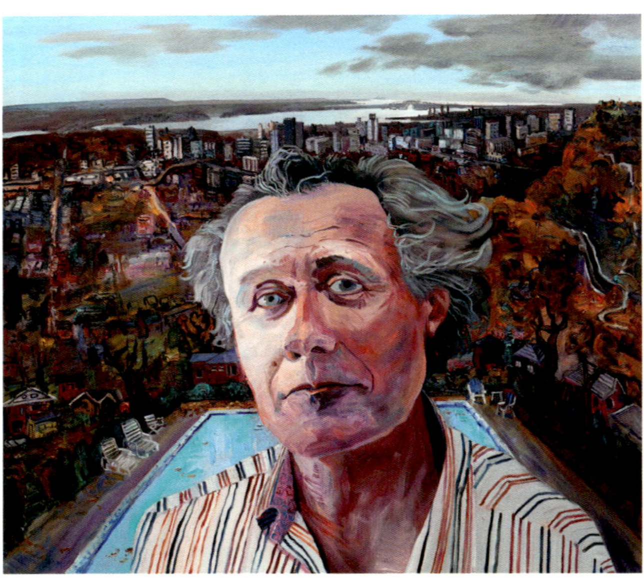

David Macfarlane above Hamilton 2014
oil on linen
60″ × 66″

explored Hamilton's escarpment and the result grew out of that experience: *David Macfarlane above Hamilton* (2014) shows the author chest up, set right against the picture plane. The landscape behind him is clearly Hamilton, and the details of the city's harbour and foliage and buildings are important. The horizon line is high, and Macfarlane's head is slightly askew, providing a sense of movement.

One of the most striking aspects of this image is how convincing it is; there is a palpable three-dimensionality and weight to Macfarlane. So too is there a tangibility and reality to the land. This is all the more remarkable when one realizes how completely artificial the composition was; it involved photographic sittings with Macfarlane and detailed landscape studies, in both watercolours and photographs (many in this project were taken with an aerial drone). Hartman brought his diverse source elements together in a compositional sketch, and only then began painting.

Of his method, he writes, "Generally, I sketched in the figure first, then I did the landscape. I painted from the top of the canvas to the bottom, in each section working from background to foreground, the landscape first then the figure. I worked on one painting at a time, not moving on until I was happy with the current canvas."

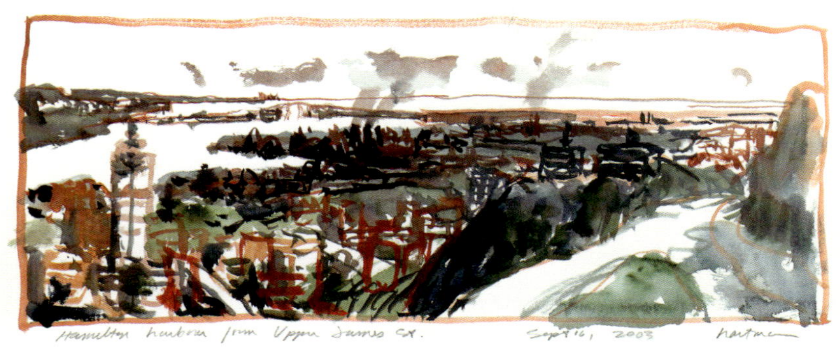

Hamilton Harbour from Upper James St. 2003
watercolour on paper
10.25″ × 14.25″

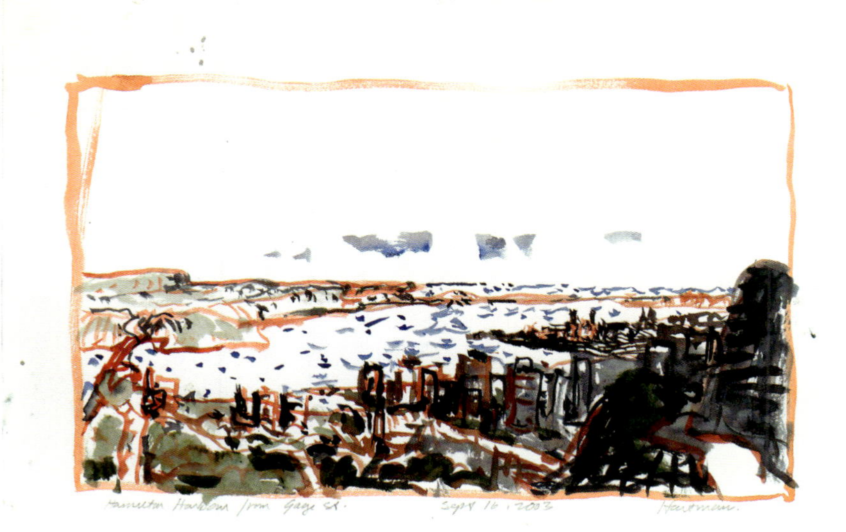

Hamilton Harbour from Gage St. 2003
watercolour on paper
10.25″ × 14.25″

The success of *David Macfarlane above Hamilton* (2014) prompted Hartman to think about connecting other writers to their landscapes. Macfarlane and others assisted the artist in compiling a list of potential subjects.

Five years later, the project has grown to more than thirty larger-than-life images, painted in 2014, 2017, 2018, and 2019. Given the technical complexity of these works, Hartman's achievement is remarkable. As he comments, "These are the most technically challenging paintings I have ever made. For them to work—for me—both the sitter and the landscape have to be recognizable. They have to appear to be effortlessly painted, and, in fact, most were effortlessly painted because of all the preparation that preceded them."

A further challenge: ensuring the ambitious project did not become formulaic. While the images all share the presence of an author and a landscape of their choosing, they come together as a remarkable mosaic of the literary and physical space of Canada. The image of *David Adams Richards above the Bartibog and Miramichi Rivers* (2018), for example, is radically different in spirit and tone from that of *Camilla Gibb above Kensington Market* (2018), but both tell us truths about the authors and their environments. This can be said of all of the portraits—from Ian Brown and Thomas King to Johanna Skibsrud and Esi Edugyan—and all of the landscapes—from Oliver, British Columbia, to Little Judique Harbour,

Cape Breton. Monumental and yet intensely human, these works have an energy and richness that reward repeated viewings.

The history of placing people within or against a landscape is a long one, but usually the landscape is a mere background. In Canadian art, for example, one might think of the work of Edwin Holgate (1892–1977), Prudence Heward (1896–1947), Lilias Torrance Newton (1896–1980), Barker Fairley (1887–1986), and Frederick Varley (1881–1969). But it was important for Hartman that his landscapes and figures be of equal gravity—that "all areas have an equal density of information," to use his words. This density, combined with the highly accomplished use of paint and colour, is what makes these works so exciting.

Hartman set out to "push the conventions of portrait painting." He has succeeded in doing so, and these pieces, building upon his previous work, are a major contribution to the history of portraiture in this country.

IAN M. THOM is a distinguished art historian and curator with more than forty years of art museum experience. He held senior curatorial positions at the Vancouver Art Gallery, Art Gallery of Greater Victoria, and McMichael Canadian Art Collection. The author of numerous books and catalogues, he was made a member of the Order of Canada in 2009.

JOHN HARTMAN

Introduction: A Hard, Bright Northern Light

MY MOST CREATIVE IDEAS seem obvious in hindsight, but they often sit with me for quite some time before I recognize them. That was certainly the case with these paintings. Two years after I completed David Macfarlane's portrait, it finally occurred to me that writers, like painters, can have strong attachments to place.

I was at a hotel in Kelowna, British Columbia, heading home after a sketching trip. I suddenly realized I could continue my exploration of people and place by painting writers in landscapes of their choosing, and I quickly began to imagine these portraits forming an exhibition. On a hotel notepad, I scribbled the names of my favourite Canadian authors, or at least those I thought might say yes to my idea. I started with people I actually knew, then fleshed out the list with those I knew only through their writing.

As soon as I got home, I began making approaches, starting with individuals who lived in Newfoundland and Labrador. Because I wanted the project to grow organically, I didn't move west until I had finished most of the portraits in that province. By then, my wish list had grown to more than thirty, although not everyone was saying yes.

I quickly developed a method for the project: I photographed authors indoors, so that they would not be squinting, with natural light coming first from one side and then the other. This would allow me to match the light on their faces with the light on the landscapes—however it came. I took a lot of shots, trying for one or two that looked and felt most like each individual. It usually took about ten minutes before they relaxed in front of my camera. If I had time, I would sketch them in watercolour, although I did most of my studies right after, referencing my best photos. The writers and I would discuss places that were important to them—a childhood haunt, a current home, a retreat that restored their creative imagination. I then visited these places, making watercolour sketches and taking aerial photos, usually from a drone but occasionally from a small plane.

Aerial perspectives allowed me to capture large geographic areas, which I tailored in the paintings to reflect an author's connection to the place. With Ian Brown's portrait, for instance, I used an aerial image taken from about one hundred feet, because he wanted me to paint him on a particular point of land at the mouth of Go Home Bay, on Georgian Bay. Katherine Govier wanted both Canmore and Banff in her painting. The imposing Mount Rundle connects these two Alberta towns, and to get it all in the painting I had to shoot from a plane at two thousand feet. In David Bergen's portrait, I wanted the confluence of the Rat and Red Rivers in the foreground, with Winnipeg on the horizon, because David told me about rafting down the Red as a teenager. I took the reference photo for that painting from an elevation of 390 feet.

In my studio, near Lafontaine, Ontario, I had to figure out how to combine the images of the writers with the landscapes of their choosing. This process could take a year, sometimes two, for each painting. It was often complicated. I photographed Michael Winter in Toronto, but he wanted Bradley's Cove in Newfoundland as the setting for his portrait. Fortunately, Michael Crummey chose Western Bay and Lisa Moore wanted Broad Cove: the three communities are minutes apart on the wild western shore of Conception Bay. Will Ferguson wanted me to paint Fort Vermilion, Alberta, where he grew up. But a November blizzard gave me second thoughts about driving eight hours from Edmonton, in a rental car without snow tires. So Will and I settled on Calgary, his current home and the setting of his novel *419*.

I began each painting only after I had a clear understanding of how I was going to join the author and the place. I wanted a balance between figure and landscape, different from conventional portraits. Instead of the latter merely filling in the empty space around the former, I wanted them to be more or less equal. My concerns about depicting the land often dictated the placement of the author. I would start by placing the subject's head lower than normal, so the

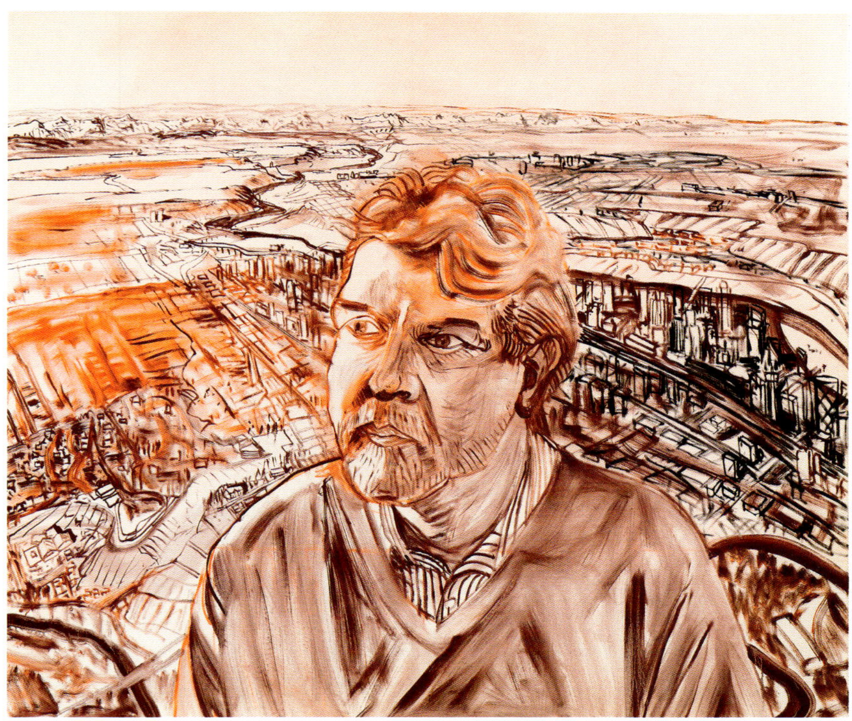

Will Ferguson above Calgary
line drawing in red paint (shown as a work in progress; final on page 99)

horizon could extend uninterrupted in the upper part of the composition. But with Susan Swan's portrait, it was crucial to include the Midland Public Library. So I painted her from the waist up, which freed space in the lower left corner.

Sometimes I made a small oil study of a writer's head, so I would know what it was like to paint him or her. I worked out my compositional ideas by drawing in ink on prints of my photos. Once I was happy with a composition, I would do a line drawing in red paint on a gessoed canvas. As I finished the paintings, one by one, I sent a digital image to each writer. Some loved how I had painted them, others were less enthusiastic, and a couple were quite upset. Since I took the view that each of us—painter and subject—had to be happy, there was the occasional repainting.

I was sure that Thomas King would pick the land west of Lethbridge, Alberta. He had taught at the university there for many years, and having listened to *The Dead Dog Café Comedy Hour* on

CBC Radio, I imagined a place somewhere between the city and the mountains. But when the time came, he said his choice was Chesterman Beach, near Tofino, British Columbia, or Guelph, Ontario, where he now lives. I decided I should go with Chesterman Beach, and I planned on three days in case of bad weather. It rained for three days. I sketched when it stopped, which it did intermittently. Finally, when I had two hours left, the weather lifted, and I could see the astounding mountains surrounding Clayoquot Sound.

Thomas says he loves this West Coast place for the way it envelops him. He says he goes to the Prairies only when he is feeling strong and invincible. He describes the land between Lethbridge and the mountains as "a bright anvil that stretches out forever under a hammered sky." But I was painting him in water-soaked Clayoquot Sound. When I made a watercolour sketch of his head and shoulders, his figure blocked much of Chesterman Beach. I decided to paint him in full figure, which allowed me to put more of the beach into the painting but left Thomas's feet floating in the sky. Around this time, I was listening to podcasts of his 2003 Massey Lectures, *The Truth about Stories: A Native Narrative*, where he would say, "There is a story I know about the earth and how it floats in space on the back of a turtle." So I painted Thomas on a turtle's back.

When I was about a quarter of the way through the project, I was heading to Go Home Bay to photograph the island Ian Brown had picked. Because I didn't want to miss anything important, I sent an email asking him to describe in more detail his connection to the place. He wrote me back a moving account of the time he spent there with his young family, many years ago. Then the penny dropped: My subjects were writers. I should be asking them to write about the places they chose.

I wrote back to the half-dozen who had already agreed to participate and asked if they would also contribute an essay. I wanted portrait and words to be parallel creative endeavours, each describing the connection between author and place, but neither illustrating the other. They all said yes.

I don't know how individuals composed their essays, and perhaps that's part of the mystery of writing. But I painted almost all the portraits in this exhibition in that sideways shining northern light: hard, bright, unforgiving. In fact, it is the light I seek in all my paintings.

I hope each of you will share Neil Bissoondath's response when he saw my painting of him for the first time: "The portrait is truly striking, and unsettling in the best possible way."

ESI EDUGYAN, VICTORIA

2018 | **oil on linen, 48″ × 54″**

IT IS NOVEMBER 2017. I am meeting Esi Edugyan at her home in Colwood, British Columbia, a western suburb of Victoria. She has asked me to paint the narrow strip of land that forms a beach between her home and Fisgard Lighthouse, at the mouth of Esquimalt Harbour. I have spent the early morning sketching and photographing the beach and the surrounding area. Esi and her partner, Steven Price, have two young children. When I arrive at their home, I am invited into a bright, minimalist living space, with no evidence of the debris that I remember following behind my children. There is original art on the walls—all portraits. I recognize a Barker Fairley.

Esi and I talk about the landscape she wants in her portrait, and I photograph her. Then she asks how I choose the one that will guide my painting. I suggest that we look at all the photos I have taken, she can flag several she's comfortable with, and I can work from that group. She is deliberate and decisive in her choices.

Esi, at this point, had won the Scotiabank Giller Prize for her book *Halfblood Blues*, which was also nominated for the Man Booker Prize, the Rogers Writers' Trust Fiction Prize, and the Governor General's Award for English-language fiction. After I finished her portrait, in 2018, she won the Giller again for *Washington Black*, her third novel. She continues to thrill and surprise us. **/JH**

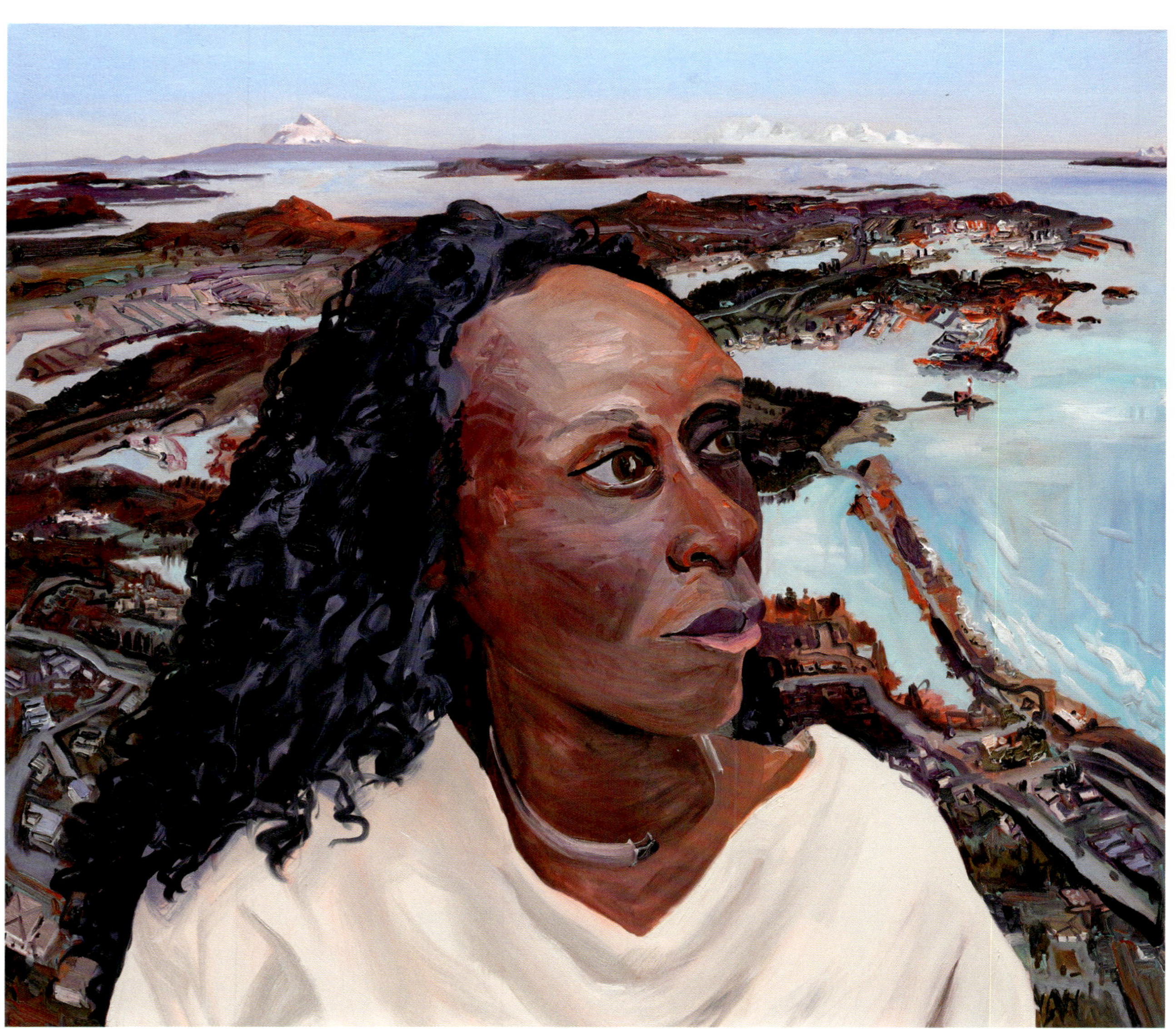

ESI EDUGYAN

Amelia's Light

TO THE RIGHT OF MY EYE, on a thinly drawn causeway snaking from the main land, sits Fisgard Lighthouse, so long a part of my days that I barely think to glance from my window. How little consideration do we spare for those things that truly anchor us. I rarely pause on the old beacon, blazing since 1860 over the sea and Esquimalt Harbour and all the surrounding lands, over the rusted artillery of Fort Rodd Hill. Yet if it were ever dismantled, I'd feel its loss intensely.

Before there was the lighthouse, there was only a single lantern burning on McLoughlin Point. A disgruntled harbourmaster placed it there, frustrated at the lack of a light to see by. Five months later, the lamp's tubes melted down from the constant heat, and it was finally decided a more permanent solution was needed. And so the bricks and stone to build the tower were locally quarried, the lens, lamp, and lantern were ferried over from England, the cast-iron spiral staircase brought north from gold-maddened San Francisco.

Of the twelve lighthouse keepers, one stands out. Amelia Bevis, the sole woman. Her husband had been keeper for eighteen years, custodian of a stillness she could scarcely imagine from the solitude of her shore life. At his sudden death, she took over, slipping into the silence of his duties as into a just-abandoned bed, the warmth still there, the smell and disorder. And she liked it. She liked it so much

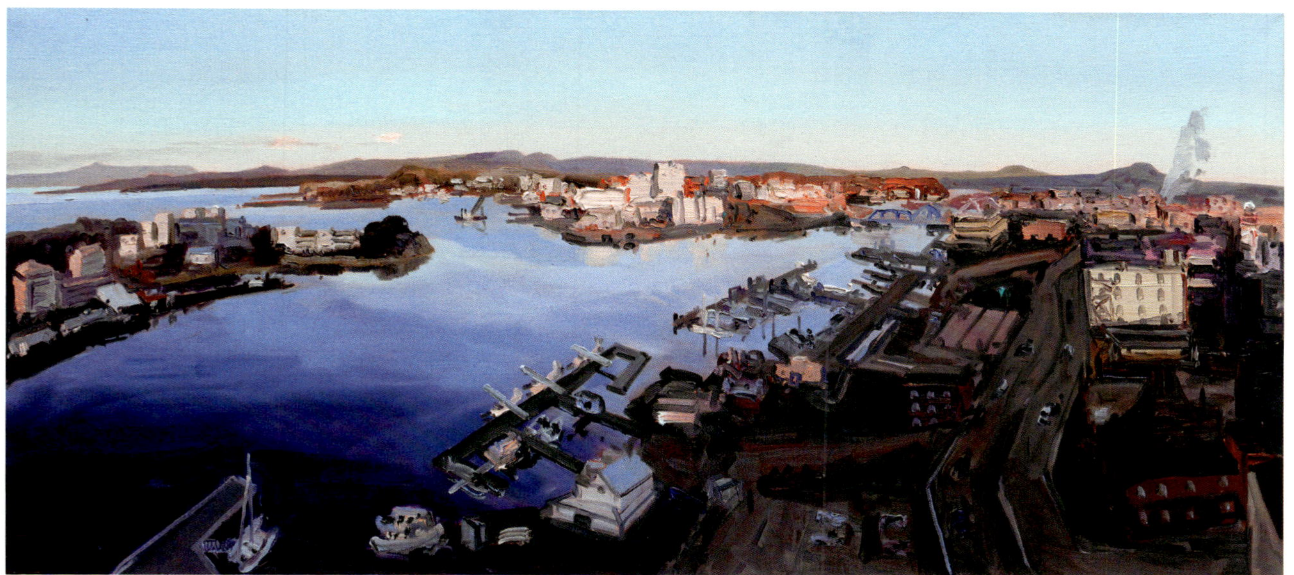

The Seaplane Base, Victoria 2018
oil on linen
22″ × 48″

that she made an application to stay in the post permanently. The response came back crisp: "It is against the rules of the Department to place Lighthouses in the charge of women."

And so she left it, this place in which the absence of her husband was something she'd worn easily, happily, in a way she had never fully managed on land. Her replacement stayed on only four years, himself replaced by a man more interested in mink hunting than guiding boats, and who one morning tripped on a rock and shot his eye out. He returned to work half-blind and drowned the following month while rowing home.

So many lives mark this place. When I do look out at the lighthouse, I see all these past joys and losses, the strangeness of lives so different from the one I share with my husband and my children on the very same shores. I peer out over the water and imagine the shudder of guns that once cracked the tower's windows, fissuring the view like some new atmospheric disturbance. And how fleeting even that small moment of consideration is—how it too will be lost. ■

NOAH RICHLER
ABOVE SANDY COVE

2018 | **oil on linen, 54″ × 48″**

NOAH RICHLER IS an author, journalist, broadcaster, and podcaster. In 2006, he published *This Is My Country, What's Yours? A Literary Atlas of Canada*, a cultural portrait of the country that used writers as a way in. It won the British Columbia National Award for Canadian Non-Fiction. I read it and loved it. In a lot of ways, the book led me to this project, some eight years later. While I had always realized that people and place inform one another, I may not have imagined painting a series of portraits of Canadian authors and the places that are important to them if I hadn't read Noah's book.

I caught up with Noah and his love, the publisher Sarah MacLachlan, in Sandy Cove, on the Digby Neck, that long finger of land that separates the Bay of Fundy and St. Marys Bay at the southwestern tip of Nova Scotia. I was there to sketch and photograph the cove. Noah and I hiked up to the height of land above the eastern entrance to the community. I made a watercolour study, and I checked out the harbour. We drove to the end of the Neck, where we had a superb seafood lunch at the diner beside the ferry. We went to the beach on the Fundy side, where Noah kept a sharp eye on anyone not conforming to the community's self-imposed garbage policy, while others baked in the July sun. I put all these places in his portrait, as they all seemed to tell a story of his attachment to this location, one he tells me would be nowhere near as strong without the people living in Sandy Cove, who keep bringing him back here. **/JH**

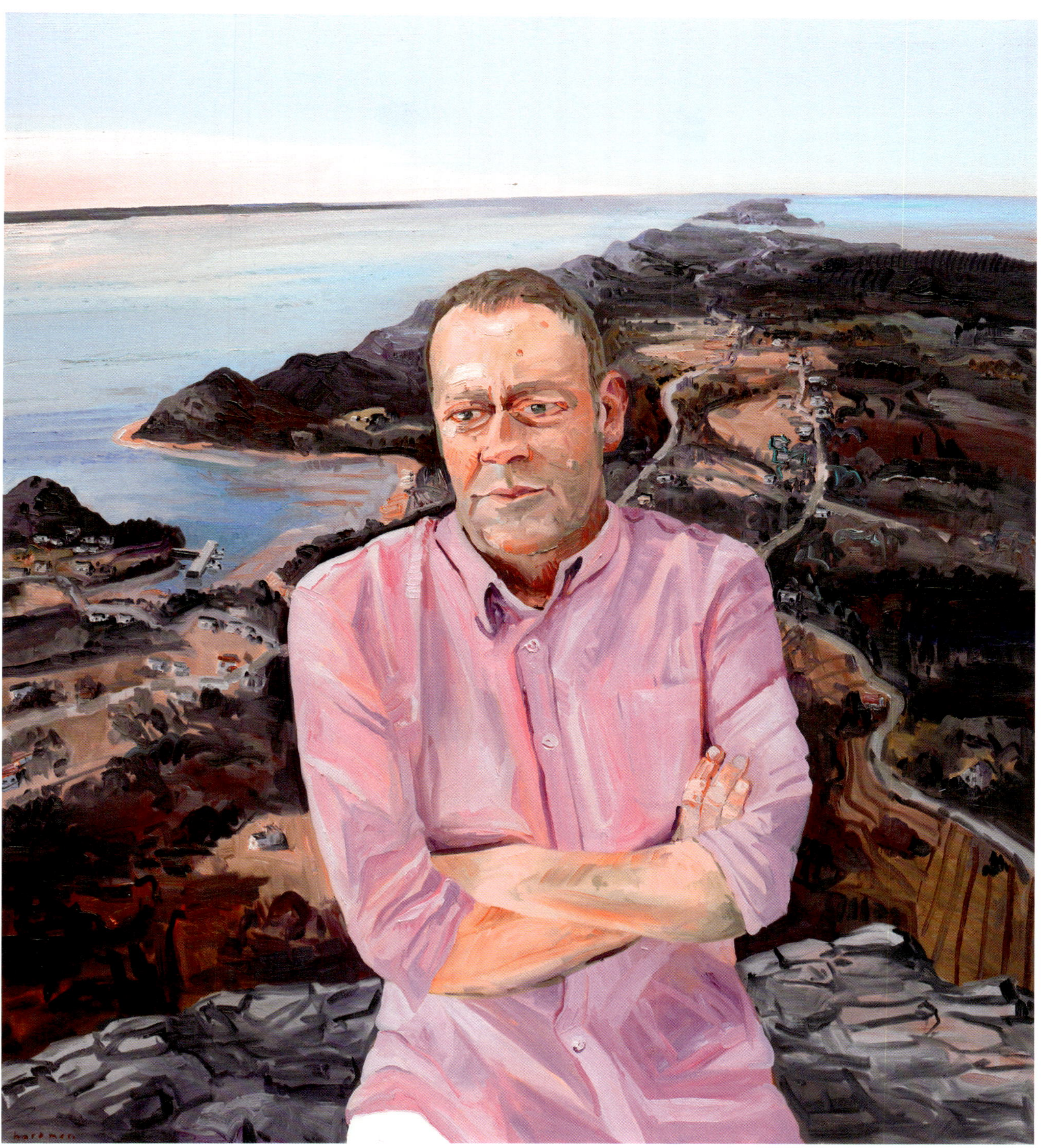

NOAH RICHLER

The Wedding Party

IT HAD BEEN RAINING for weeks before the Saturday in Sandy Cove when Jen and Paul were to be married. The long peninsula of Digby Neck and Islands is at its thinnest here, less than a kilometre from St. Marys Bay to the wilder Bay of Fundy shore. Some days there's a downpour on one side while on the other the sky is perfectly clear, but today it was raining on both sides and folk were worried. Paul Gidney, you see, was the Cove's favourite son. The last in a line of several generations of lobster fishers, he'd decided, early on, that lobstering was not for him; he'd become a gardener and a vegan, though never the proselytizing sort. Paul had never flown on a plane and rarely left the village because, he said, reading was enough. He'd been the fancy of many of the women visiting each summer, some of whose families had been coming up since United Empire Loyalist days, so you'll understand if his romance with Jen Ritchie, a childhood friend lately returned, caught them by surprise. You could feel the blunt of their longing, but also that the women—sometimes a mother *and* her daughter—knew how absurdly proprietorial they were being. Now was the time to think of *his* happiness, not theirs.

Everyone wanted the best for Jen and Paul, and today that meant *sun*. Geanna dressed up as a pig in a pink tutu and led a sun dance with her friends on the hill overlooking St. Marys, unsure whose mythology spawned the ritual. Over by Fundy, the tables and the tents went up. The band was rehearsing and the cooks and guests had arrived, waiting by Paul and Jen's bountiful flower and vegetable garden, any takers welcome, and looking to the top of the field for the couple to appear. Anxiously: cold grey sky overhead, rain still spitting. But Geanna's dance must have worked, because suddenly gold shafts of sunlight broke through the dark cloud cover and Jen and Paul appeared, the whites of their shirts catching the full blaze of the sun and the pair descending hand-in-hand down the hill and through the lush field.

Everyone was there: the Gidneys and the Ritchies, the Cunninghams, the Montins, the Tidds, the Trasks, and the Walkers, all the generations. Chook Smith—in his eighties now but, in his teens, a hockey player from Windsor who'd missed family too much and skipped the NHL to be home—was sashaying as much as the grass allowed and twirling fortysomething Sarah by the arm. Steve, Penny, and Josh, rarely seen outside the K-Way, were approving sentinels in attendance, and Geanna, out of costume now, was ladling out the chowder. Her Larry, hard-of-hearing when it suited, was well turned out and standing with their grown-up fisher sons. Young Genevieve, Broadway the dream, was at the mic now, little though she needed it. And there was Roger, the gentle lilt of his speaking like an Atlantic spoken-word lullaby, and a bevy of laughing children chasing and being chased and tumbling at it-didn't-matter-which adult's feet.

A place without stories is just a landscape, a Cape Breton writer friend once said to me, and whose story wasn't here? Really, how many people do you have to know? ■

KATHLEEN WINTER
ABOVE VERDUN

2018 | **oil on linen, 60″ × 66″**

KATHLEEN WINTER LIVES in Verdun, as close to the St. Lawrence River as is possible in this Montreal neighbourhood of two- and three-storey flats. Between her place and the river, there is a mixture of new municipal parks and much older industrial buildings and yards. Just to the east, behind Kathleen in the painting, the city is busy rebuilding the multi-lane highway that cuts south and crosses the wide span of the river. In the painting's lower right corner, there is a strip of wild land—or, rather, neglected land—at the water's edge, with two walking paths, one below and one above the riverbank, the lower of which appears to have been created by desire rather than design. In one spot, abandoned sleeping bags, cardboard shelters, and a fire pit delineate a camp for homeless people.

Kathleen is perhaps best known for *Annabel*, her award-winning novel set in Labrador, but I am thinking of her new novel, *Lost in September*, whose war veteran protagonist, Jimmy, camps out on the streets in Montreal. **/JH**

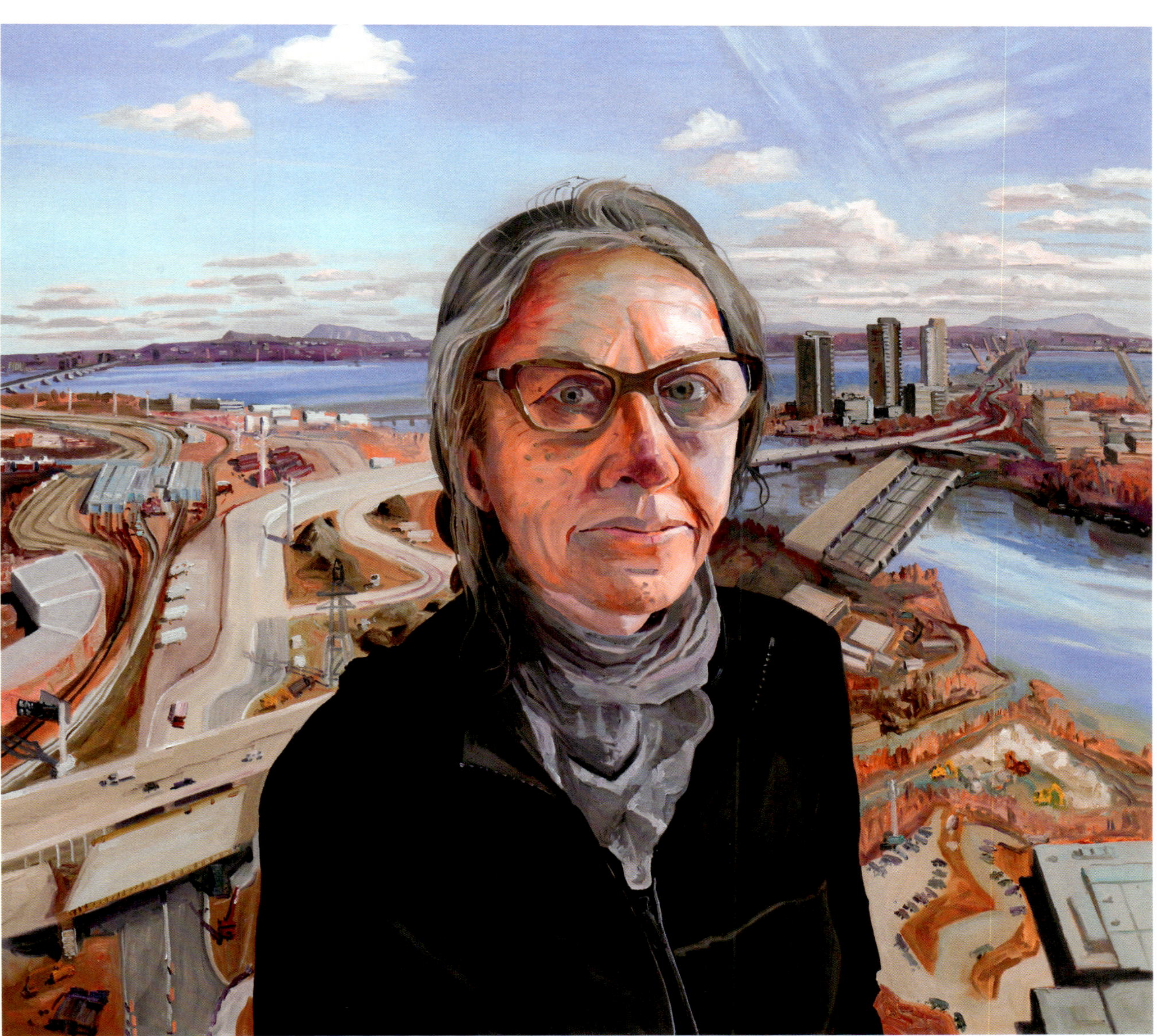

KATHLEEN WINTER

The Frayed Edge

THE FRAYED EDGE of the St. Lawrence has bulrushes, sumac, orphaned lilacs, and a walnut tree. I go to the river and visit ducks and herons. The wild black cherries make thick jam, but red-winged blackbirds dive-bomb your head. I take Hunk and Merlin down there for walks. I've peed in the bushes and swum naked. I'm not the only one. The river hem is hardly a wild place, but the river is muscular and ice sparkles in winter. I've lain on it in blazing sun.

My apartment, two minutes away, has vines and a linden and a purple balcony where we eat and hear the neighbours murmur. There are children and communal cats, raccoons and squirrels. The man next door yelled on his front step every night until he was murdered. We have a shiitake log propped on the fence but no mushrooms yet. The Korean restaurant on the corner of Edna and LaSalle twice-fries chicken and paints it with spicy sauce. I have a hard time not ordering some every Friday night.

Men play electric guitars on the steps of Our Lady of Seven Sorrows. A woman asks for money for lipstick. My husband is enchanted by her smile.

The noise is getting unbearable. At first it was only sirens and traffic. I got used to it the way I once got used to having a rooster. Now Montreal is using jackhammers to tear up rue Ross behind us, and Verdun Hospital in front of us is getting a new pavilion. Men were there at seven this morning with chainsaws to remove the sumac and cedars, and a forklift to put up fourteen sets of scaffolding. Street painters painted new lines at our intersection all last night, hollering. Vehicles hurtle past at four in the morning bearing spans for the new Champlain Bridge being built just along the river. Those vehicles are more than a city block long, and their multiple wheels are not wheels so much as gigantic rollers. The bridge affair has a police car escort fore and aft, and our triplex shakes. It's so hot you have to open the windows, but the racket is brutal. I have a pair of Honeywell-certified Australian-standard ear protectors that don't help.

A few months ago, developers put up a tent and invited locals in for miniature Angus burgers, beet and feta kebabs, and tiny éclairs, while they used PowerPoint to explain forthcoming condos. We cleaned the developers right out of food—the lipstick lady and electric guitarists, myself and other bush-peeing, river-traipsing residents. When they invited questions, someone wanted to know if there would be a cinema to replace the Palace Theatre lost many years ago. The developers seemed surprised, and did not know anything about a lost cinema. There might not be a cinema, they said, but there would be a small border of grass around the condos that all of us would be welcome, within reason, to enjoy. ■

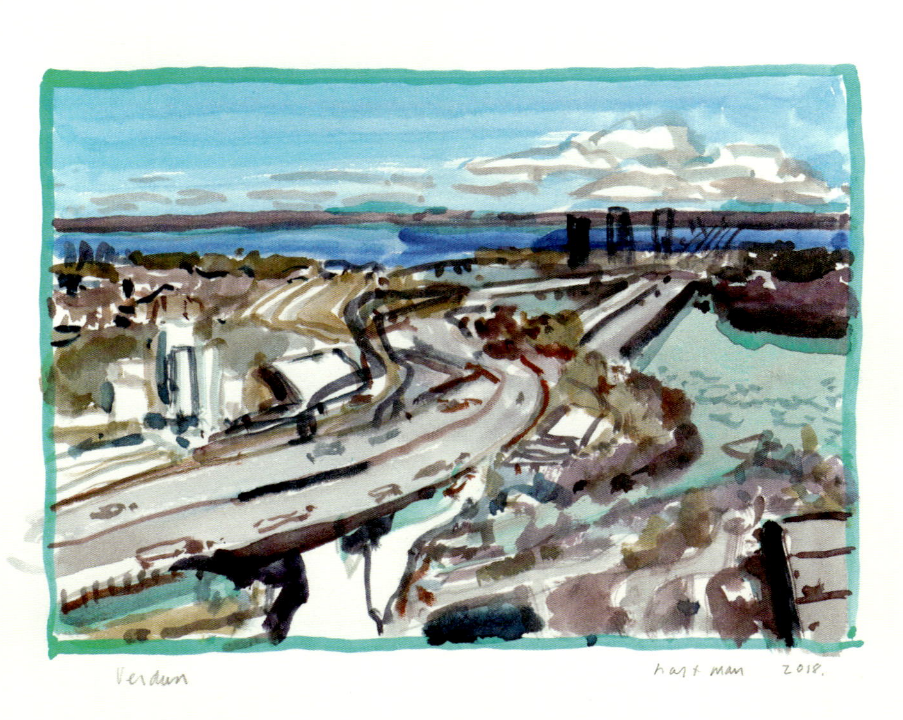

Verdun 2018
watercolour on paper
9.25″ × 11.25″

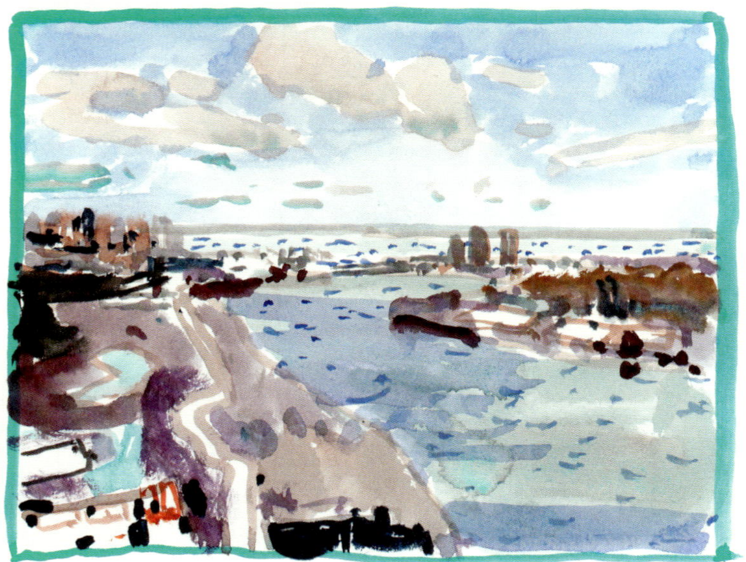

Verdun and the St. Lawrence 2018
watercolour on paper
9.25″ × 11.25″

THOMAS WHARTON ABOVE THE HOOKER ICEFIELD

2018 | **oil on linen, 48″ × 54″**

I BEGAN TO understand how to paint the Rocky Mountains as I read Thomas Wharton's award-winning novel *Icefields* for the first time. I was travelling from Banff to Jasper on the Icefields Parkway, making tiny pencil drawings of mountains. Glaciation intrigues me. Thomas, too, is fascinated with the melting and retreat of glaciers. It is a central idea in the book.

Thomas and I seem to share a sense of awe of the mountains, but we are quick to point out that our experiences are limited when compared to storied mountain people like Jimmy Simpson or Chic Scott. Thomas lived in Jasper from age fifteen to eighteen, and these were the years that formed his core experience of the mountains. He has rarely been far away from them, having been born in Grande Prairie and studied in Edmonton. He now teaches at the University of Alberta, and lives in the countryside just east of the city.

I have painted Thomas above the Hooker Icefield, near the point where Mount Hooker pokes its peak out of the glacier, which spills out its layers of rock, ice, and small traces of human histories into the valley of the Whirlpool River. **/JH**

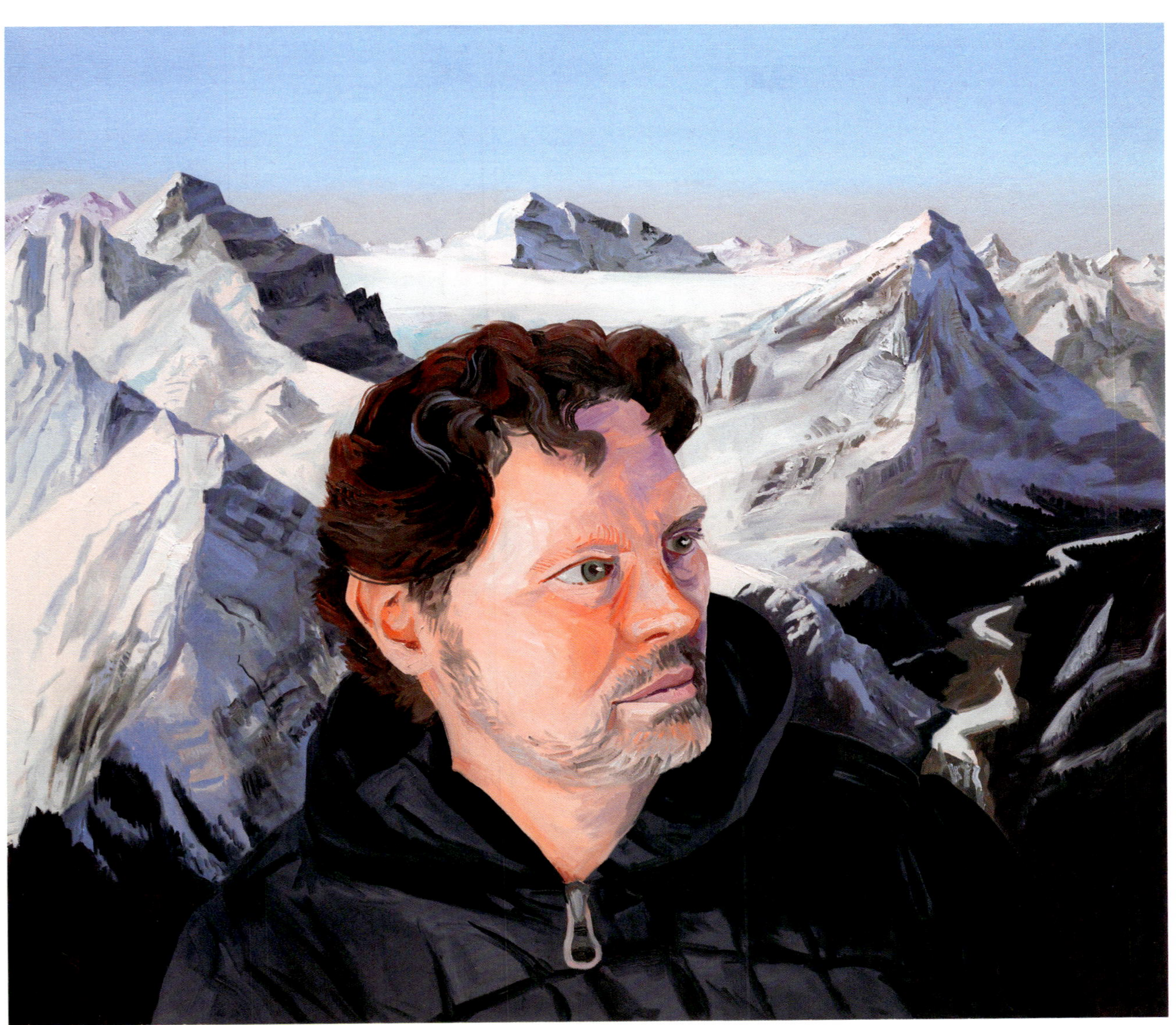

THOMAS WHARTON

The Country of Illumination

THE PAINTING DEPICTS the Whirlpool River valley and Mount Brown, long misidentified on early maps of the region as by far the highest peak in the Canadian Rockies, a fabled colossus of purportedly Himalayan stature. Until someone finally did a proper survey and shaved several thousand feet off the mountain's height. This kind of fabulation isn't surprising to anyone who has spent time in the region. The endlessly folding and unfolding mountain terrain, with its sudden chasms and looping rivers, plays tricks with one's perception of height and distance. And the stories that mountain dwellers tell usually start out big and tend to get larger and more elaborate over time. This is why Jasper novelist Howard O'Hagan called the Rockies "the country of illusion." For me it's also the country of illumination.

I moved to Jasper, Alberta, with my family when I was fifteen, and the mountains forever altered both my inner and outer worlds. It was the perfect landscape for a shy, broody teenager to lose himself in, and I did, spending countless hours prowling the woods and hills around our home, imagining myself in some other world—Middle-earth, or an uncharted planet I was the first to explore. With friends from high school, I went on unforgettable multi-day excursions into the high country, scrambled up rock faces, climbed down into canyons of ice. I think back on our lack of preparation and training for some of these escapades and marvel that we survived our own stupidity.

I was also fortunate enough to hear first-hand some of the tales of local raconteurs like Willi Pfisterer, the legendary alpine guide. I ate up the tall tales and spooky legends of the Rockies, not suspecting that years later I would draw on this rich vein of lore for my first novel, *Icefields*. Of course, there was also a girl, an unattainable beauty transmuted many years later into the daughter of the town's patrician doctor in my collection of linked stories, *The Logogryph*. The mountains are indelibly part of me now, an endlessly shifting but enduring map of memory and longing.

I love the mountain parks in all their moods and weathers, but the landscape that has always drawn me most powerfully is the alpine tundra of bare and broken rock, wind, fierce light, and ice. For me, glaciers are uncanny beings of intertwined opposites: solidity and flow, profound stillness and constant movement, tumbling stones and trickling streams, deep silence and a ceaseless music of creaks and groans. At your feet, a wall of ancient water turning into a river, rejoining time and mutability.

Maybe that's why I so often write about those moments when one thing becomes something else. When things change their skin and reveal themselves to be other, or more, than what they seemed to be. I look for a contrast, an edge, a border, a boundary. I start writing there, and the boundary opens up and reveals a dynamic, fluid, elusive reality I can only attempt to trace with words. ■

MEGAN COLES
ABOVE SAVAGE COVE

2018 | **oil on linen, 48″ × 54″**

MEGAN GAIL COLES is from Savage Cove on the Great Northern Peninsula of Newfoundland. If you keep following the highway, it soon swings to the eastern side of the peninsula, to the larger community of St. Anthony and the reconstructed Viking community at L'Anse aux Meadows. It is a low, rocky coast, hammered by winds that blow across the Strait of Belle Isle from Labrador.

There is an older road, which hugs the coast more closely, and it is here that a young Megan would "walk making up stories and talking to myself." She points out, "It is barren windswept bog. Super salty and too rugged for conversation."

Megan now lives in St. John's, but she travels regularly to Savage Cove, a twelve-hour drive. It seems like she brings Savage Cove with her wherever she goes, so I painted her house with wings flying above the harbour.

Megan is well-known as a playwright, and is the co-founder and artistic director of Poverty Cove Theatre Company. She is also the executive director of Riddle Fence, a literary journal. In 2014, she won the Winterset Award for *Eating Habits of the Chronically Lonesome*, a short story collection, and she's just published a novel, *Small Game Hunting at the Local Coward Gun Club*. **/JH**

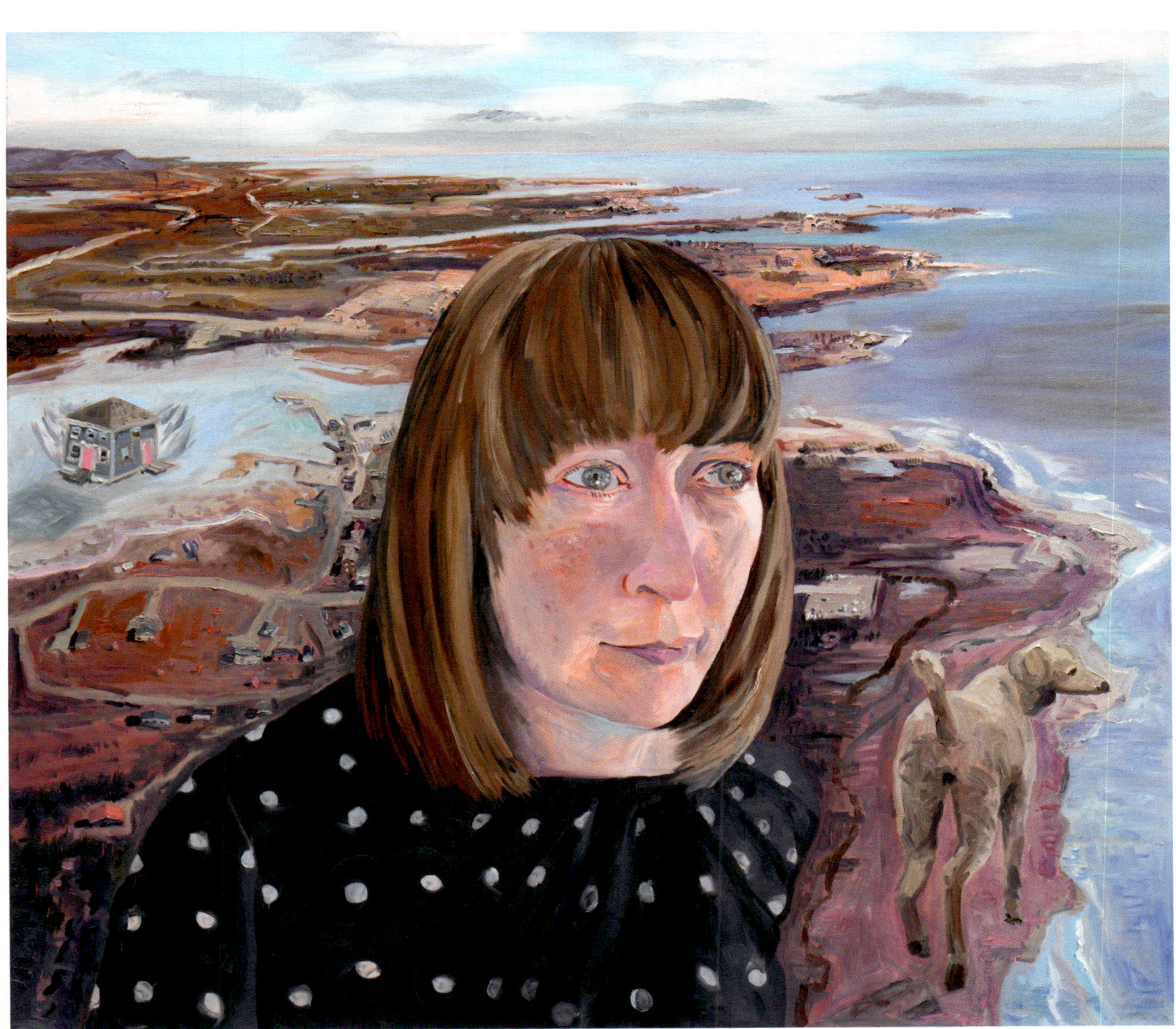

MEGAN GAIL COLES

Salt Stained Through

HERE IS A PART of the story you don't know.

I did not inherit my grandmother's house from my grandmother. It was left to the estate. My father and his siblings, spread across Newfoundland and the country, were willed the worth of it. Though they hadn't privilege enough to care for the beloved shell of our bygone livelihoods, as they were far too furious with the busy work of living. Revolving economic disasters steady occupied the passing of their growing adult days. They kept the lights on, they kept the truck going. We were reared up smart and sturdy Coles, as the gale force wind and freezing rain went on lashing Nanny's house.

We lost track of each other in the time shift, moved further afield by out-migration, education, determination, even death. And as we ebbed and flowed from the cove, the tides turned over. Our family home fell into disrepair. We watched it falling. We took pictures of the fallen bits upon the firm and frozen ground. Documenting pieces of ourselves like paint chips peeling from the clapboard. The porch, having blown open one winter, smelled of wet rot. Our school photos still hung in frames on the warped papered walls. What a sin, we said, what a sin for us. Cousins whispered about the state of it while drinking beers under blankets on the couch. There were murmurs amongst the older lot. The house, they said, would have to be torn down.

So I asked for it.

From Montreal, I wrote a letter. I begged my elders for the little biscuit box out on the point. I was twenty-five and penniless. I told them one day I would be neither and we would all wish after Nanny's sitting room then. What do you want that for, Meggie, they wondered aloud, worried that I was wading in over my boots. Me—their well-known and much-loved boot-soaker. But they gave me my way. And Dad allowed me to foreman us into my thirties, tearing the tiny house back to her studs. Frantically gathering up small pockets of funds, progress always held up by my bank account. This year, the doors and windows. Next year, the siding. Electrical upgrades are some dear. In and out of the poor house strutted my stubborn nature. And there were times when I thought, What have you done? When I thought, You are held here now. When I thought, This is much too much rowing with your father.

But I did what I did because I knew then as I do now that I have always been held to this present rowing over the past to make up the future with my father. That we are bound to the cove and to each other and to the whole of our fierce family like carbon fast-fixed in the rough rock we survive upon. And I am so proud of these people who somehow made themselves up on this point nine miles from the mainland, always facing Canada but a world away.

So it is that when I am heart-hurt, wounded, or weary, when I forget myself and feel afraid, I drive an entire day's length to Savage Cove. The place where I made myself up, too. And I sleep in my little blue bedroom, in my little green house, so I can wake to the same crisp morning light that woke my grandmother. I do this to remember her, myself, who we are, and who we can be on our Great Northern Peninsula. ■

THOMAS KING ABOVE CHESTERMAN BEACH

2018 | **oil on linen, 66″ × 60″**

THOMAS KING LIVES in Guelph, Ontario, in a home that he designed, close to the Speed River, which bisects the city's downtown. He is nationally known and admired as a writer and broadcaster. *The Inconvenient Indian: A Curious Account of Native People in North America* won the RBC Taylor Prize in 2014. Between 1997 and 2000, he wrote and acted in the CBC Radio show *The Dead Dog Café Comedy Hour*. When I visited him at his home, he reminded me that he had a career as a professional photographer as well.

But it was Chesterman Beach, near Tofino, on Vancouver Island, that was Thomas's first choice for his landscape. This is closer to the setting of his novel *The Back of the Turtle*, though his pick seemed more personal to me. I have painted him above the peninsula that ends at Tofino, projecting into Clayoquot Sound. Chesterman Beach runs from the left foreground to just behind his right shoulder. Frank Island, a mass of black rock, sits a little offshore in the middle of the beach and breaks the waves in such a way that they form the two broad crescent-shaped beaches that compose Chesterman. The turtle that Thomas is standing on, the otter, and the twins all come from stories that he told in his 2003 CBC Massey Lectures, published as *The Truth about Stories: A Native Narrative*. **/JH**

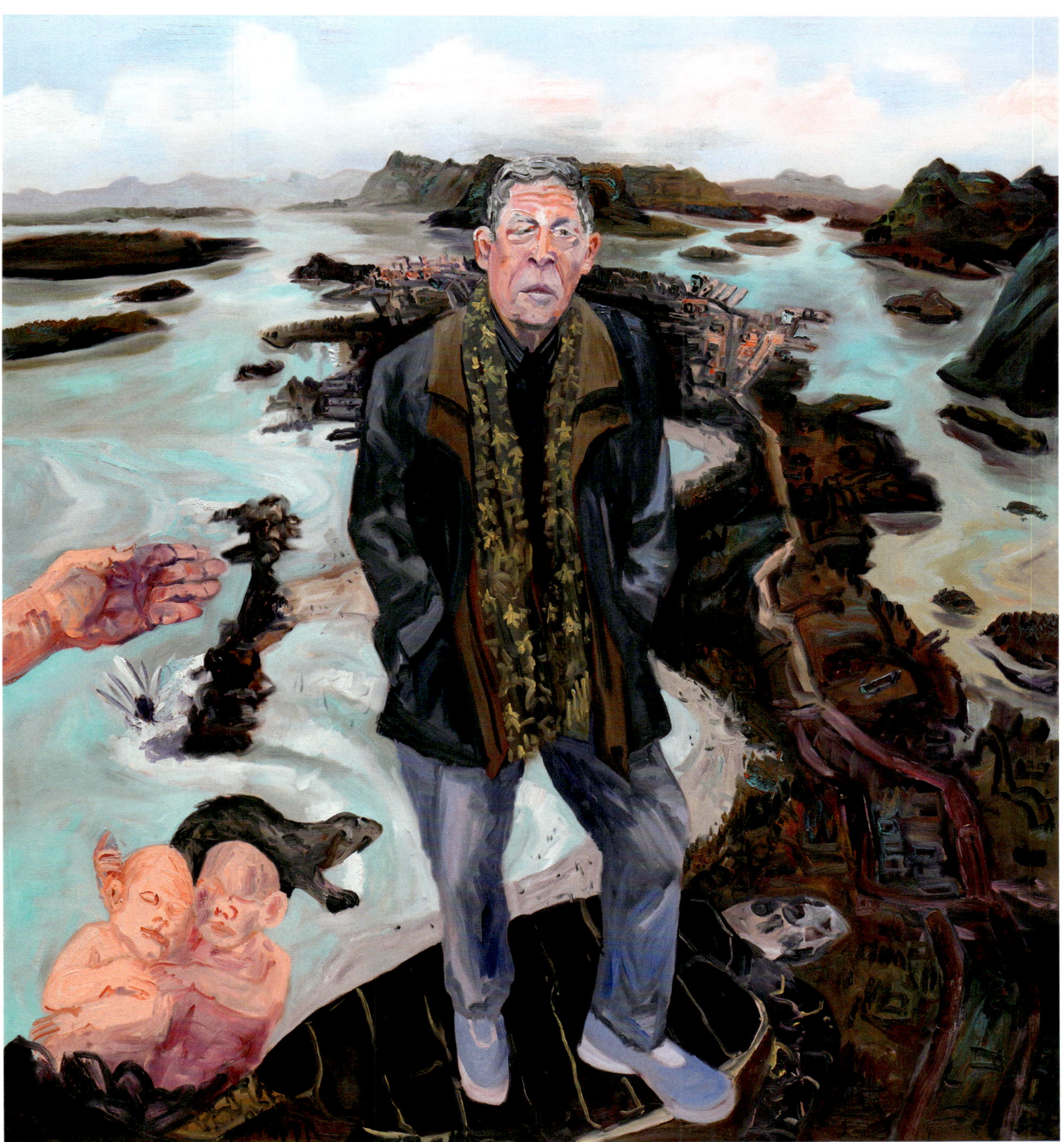

THOMAS KING

The Line between Worlds

I'VE ALWAYS BEEN DRAWN to the coast. It's a magical place where two worlds meet.

Land and water.

And there's no better spot on Canada's west coast than the area around Tofino. Wet. Gloomy. Even on sunny days, the fog is never far away. Step into the Rhino café on Campbell Street for a cup of coffee, and by the time you come out, all of creation is once again gray and melancholic.

Perfect.

In this part of the world, it's always light-jacket-and-heavy-shirt weather. And rain. Land's edge on the western ocean is a haven for rain. And then there are the tides.

We were on Long Beach once during a particularly low tide, had walked out across the flats to where the sand had been carved into deep valleys by the retreating water. We had started in sunshine, but were overtaken by a dense fog that had sneaked in behind us. We could hardly see beyond our hands, and, suddenly, we found ourselves in an alien world, blind and lost.

A dark Mars.

Our first thought was the kids. They had wandered off, as kids will do, and now we had no idea where they were. We couldn't wait for the fog to lift because there was no promise that it would. And besides, the tide wasn't going to stay away forever. At some point soon, it would return, would rise up and drown the land. So we began a rather lame game of Marco Polo, shouting out their names, searching for them in the darkness.

Oddly enough, I wasn't worried, but I did wonder if coastal weather somehow insulated the world from sound, wondered whether Benjamin and Elizabeth were trying to find us as we were trying to find them, our voices swallowed up by the fog and the surf, whole and complete.

When I'm feeling strong and invincible, I go to the Prairies and stand in the sun. The land between Waterton and Lethbridge is spectacular. But it is not for the meek. It's a bright anvil that stretches out forever under a hammered sky.

Whereas the coast is a lonely refuge, a soft blanket, a gentle lover.

The fog eventually lifted, and we found the kids. They hadn't been concerned. For them it had been just another of those adventures, the sort only the young can appreciate. But by then, the tide had turned, forcing us further and further up the sand until the retreat became a game, an exercise in balance. And we walked all the way back to our cabin with one foot in the water and the other on land.

Perfect.

The coast. The magical place where two worlds meet. ■

LINDEN MACINTYRE ABOVE LITTLE JUDIQUE HARBOUR

2018 | **oil on linen, 60″ × 66″**

LINDEN MACINTYRE HAS a fierce attachment to Little Judique Harbour and its people, mostly the MacDonalds, who keep their fishing boats there. His summer home is a few kilometres down the road from the harbour—a farmhouse on the edge of a hayfield that fronts onto a tidal pond. Linden grew up in Port Hastings, Cape Breton, thirty-six kilometres from Little Judique, and although he is certainly not a tourist here, I suspect he is not seen as a local either. He seems comfortable with this status.

Linden has had a very successful career and is widely respected: He won many awards for the investigative reports he wrote and narrated for the CBC's *The Fifth Estate*. The second novel of his Cape Breton Trilogy, *The Bishop's Man*, won the 2009 Scotiabank Giller Prize.

I photographed him in the wheelhouse of his boat. I then photographed the harbour with a drone, looking north from above. I don't think that Linden had a sunburn that day, or even a noticeable tan, but the light in the boat made his face look red. I left it that way when I painted him. His boat is the one moored on the lower side of the harbour, right behind his shoulder. **/JH**

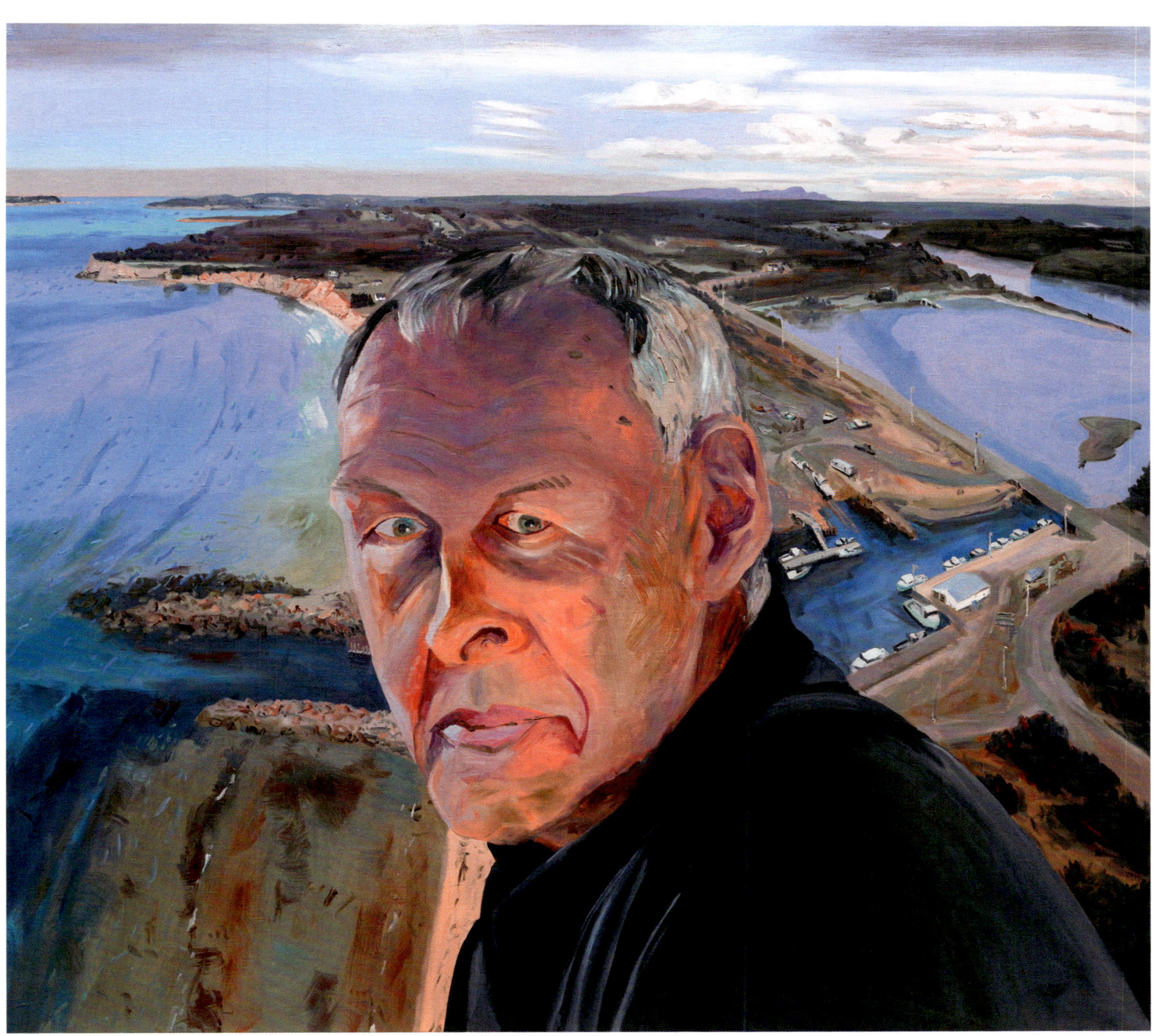

LINDEN MACINTYRE

A Haven

FROM THE GROUND it looks exactly like a harbour. There is deep water. There are buildings and docks. There are boats tied to those docks.

But from the air over Cape Breton, you realize it's not quite a harbour after all. It is a narrow channel leading to a broad and useless tidal estuary. I say "useless" because the estuary is so shallow that it becomes a mud flat when the tide withdraws.

Functionally, the outer space does serve a purpose. It offers shelter from the sea and wind, a place to safely store the necessities for fishing and, for mariners like me, summer recreation.

But it is not an easy place to drive a boat.

In most harbours, the tidal action is gently up and down. Here, because of that vast, shallow estuary, the tidal flow is also back and forth with notorious velocity—which causes navigational perils more common in a river than a harbour.

I learned of this peculiarity the first time I tried to tie a boat up here. I then spent many years coming to terms with what the local fishermen told me: we cannot win a war with our environment.

Survival is to quickly figure out what the current (or the wind) is doing, and then to submit to nature's will and whim. There is no other way.

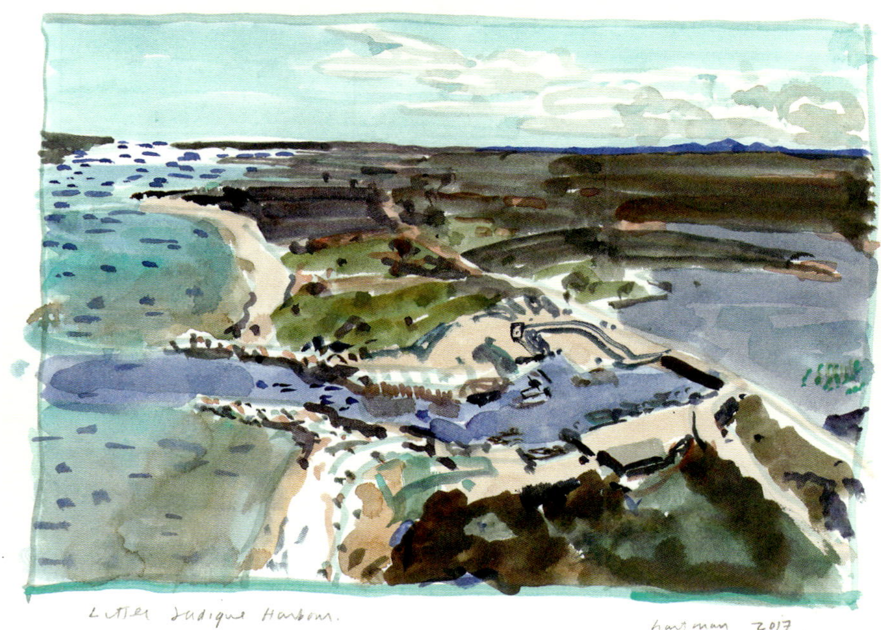

Little Judique Harbour 2017
watercolour on paper
9″ × 11.25″

A simple notion, but it took me nearly thirty years to learn how to read, and then respond to, the aggressive moods of Little Judique Harbour. Thirty years' memory inscribed indelibly by moments of raw terror and humiliation.

About twenty years ago, some distant bureaucrats decided that there were too many harbours in the area—three in the space of a mere eight kilometres. Two had to go, and this quirky place was one of them. Good, I thought. Long overdue.

I assumed that, like me, the other users of the harbour—including a dozen or so fishermen—would welcome a more congenial environment.

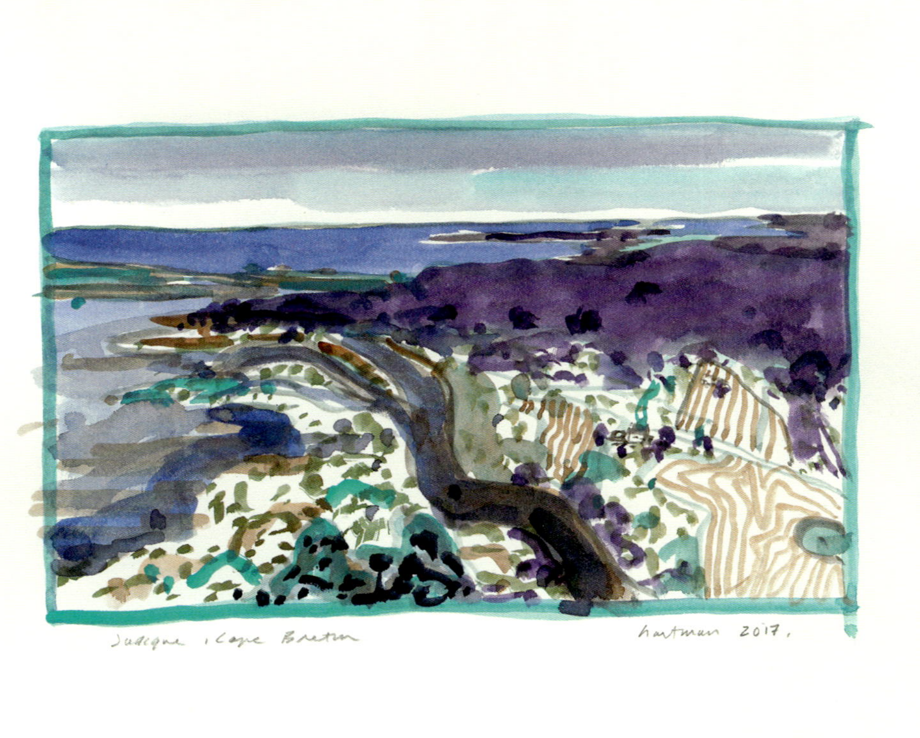

Judique, Cape Breton 2017
watercolour on paper
9″ × 11.25″

I was thinking of the tides, the current, the constant battle with the implacable will of Mother Nature. I neglected the more important issue: tradition. That the dozen fishing families for whom this place was livelihood had long ago, under the direction of their dads and granddads and great-granddads, come to terms with nature and learned to use the tide as energy, as nature's muscle, to help control their boats.

Little Judique Harbour was a haven. And would remain one. Bureaucracy or not.

The people saw no reason for a change, and so, using the predictable and vivid language of the sea, they refused to leave.

The politicians and bureaucrats persisted. The harbour, officially, ceased to exist.

But the people stayed, and as they have done for more than a century, they continue using Little Judique Harbour.

I stayed with them.

I persisted in the challenge that has defined three decades for me: To learn to work with nature. To let nature help me drive my boat. A boat that is part of nature. That is secretly on nature's side. You cannot win a fight with Mother Nature and a boat.

And after all those years, I have been rewarded by the knowledge that the arrival of my boat no longer causes people working in Little Judique Harbour to watch with expressions of dismay.

I come. I go. They pause briefly, glance, maybe nod. They resume their chores or their ongoing conversations about the absent cod, the wily tuna, the constant lobster.

My victory in nature is that my arrival in Little Judique Harbour is no longer interesting. ■

MARINA ENDICOTT ABOVE THE FOOTHILLS WEST OF COCHRANE

2018 | **oil on linen, 40″ × 46″**

MARINA ENDICOTT IS the daughter of an Anglican priest. She was born in Golden, British Columbia, and grew up with her family in Vancouver, Halifax, Yarmouth, and Toronto. As an adult, she has lived in London, England; Saskatoon, Saskatchewan; and Edmonton, Cochrane, and Mayerthorpe, Alberta. She is married to Peter Ormshaw, a Mountie and a poet. Such is the itinerant life of priests and policemen, and their children and partners.

When I asked Marina which place she would like in her portrait, she suggested the land west of Cochrane. Among other things, she said she loved the way it undulated like waves about to crash against the wall of the Rocky Mountains.

Marina worked as an actor and theatre director before she changed course and began to write fiction. Her last three novels have all been longlisted for the Scotiabank Giller Prize; her novel *Good to a Fault* was shortlisted in 2008, and won the 2009 Commonwealth Writers' Prize. **/JH**

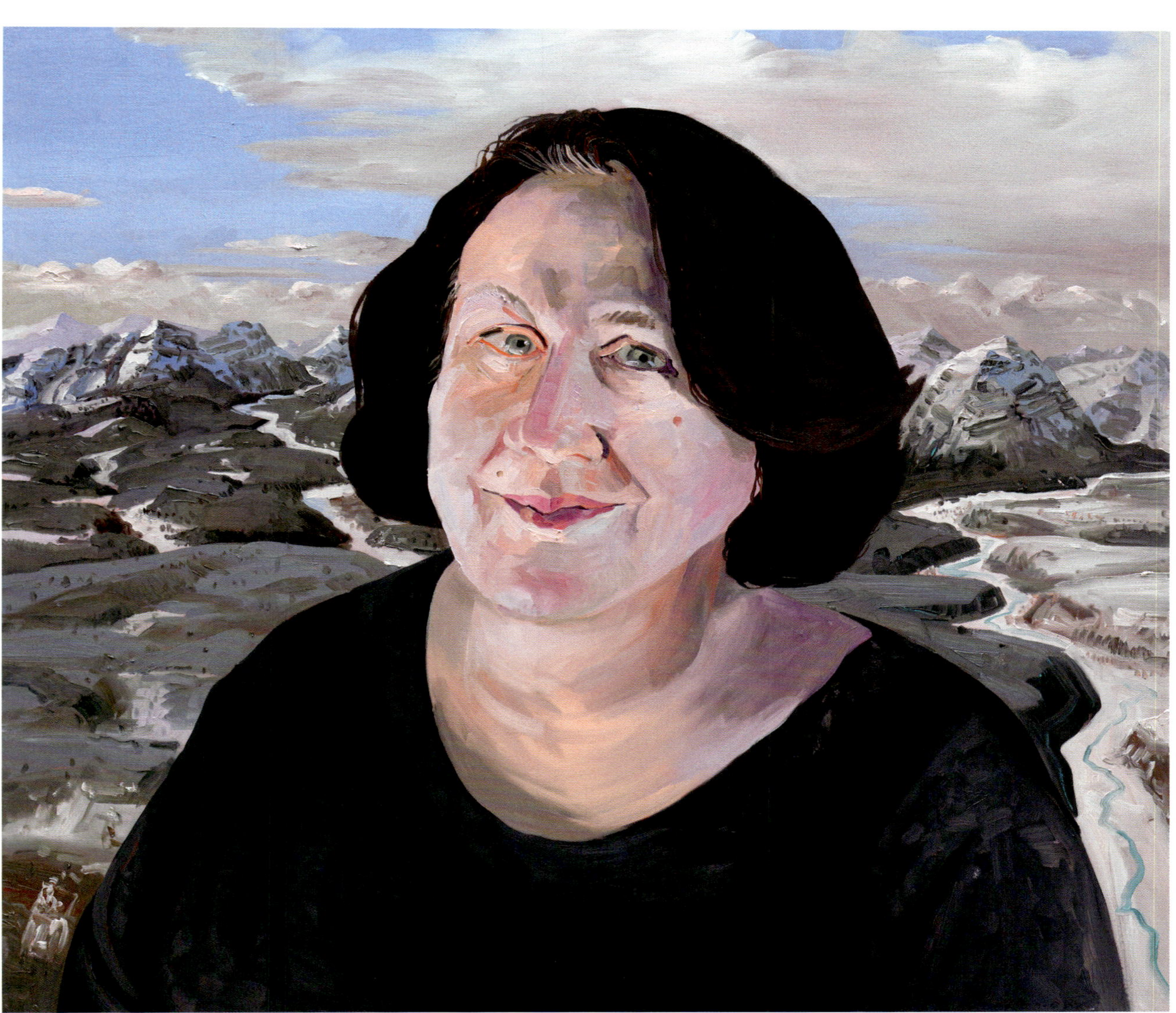

MARINA ENDICOTT

The Preamble

EVERY DAY I WAS GRATEFUL for the sweep of the beautiful land around Cochrane, Alberta. The hill above the town, high enough that hang-gliders soar there all summer, gave a novelist's perspective to the view. Everything unfolded below you, river and rocks and lives revealed and open to the eye.

No matter how hard things got there, and they were often hard as I scrambled to make a freelance living and maintain peace at home for my RCMP husband, the bare hills and the river made it easier to continue. Before we were posted to Cochrane, I wrestled with fiction while doing other work and having babies; while we were there, my children began to grow up, allowing me to concentrate on writing for more than four minutes at a time and to see the world partly through their new eyes.

One day when things were horrible, I put the children in the car and drove to Banff, an hour away, where I climbed Tunnel Mountain. I was going to leave, this was impossible, I would find a motel and make some plans. But my sturdy daughter, not yet two, and my stalwart four-year-old son climbed with me, happy to be in the woods. We stood on the peak and—oh well, you know, the mountains make you feel better. And who cares, that was Then, this was the irretrievable Now.

So we climbed down and went home. Instead of leaving, I buckled down and wrote and rewrote, got a novel published and wrote another one, started a reading program and writing workshops, found some good writers to talk to. Whenever my own writing weighed me down, I went out into that unadorned landscape, where you can see the bones of the earth and the structure of things, and I felt better.

The mountains are good, but there's a lot to be said for their preamble, the foothills, as they rise step by step into the great magnificence. The hills are attainable, even for someone who doesn't like to walk; they lead you up into the heights one ordinary pace at a time, without letting you lose sight of the small details of path and grass and bird.

Transcendence is that feeling of God-above-us, superior and removed. Approaching Cochrane from the east, you experience transcendence, looking down from above, descending into the world. But down in the river flat, there is the corresponding and equally valuable feeling of immanence, of God-with-us, that everything around you is filled with radiant meaning, that we are all part of one thing, a thing worth making. Good news for a novelist. ■

GUY VANDERHAEGHE
ABOVE SASKATOON

2018 | **oil on linen, 60″ × 66″**

GUY VANDERHAEGHE WAS born and raised in Esterhazy, Saskatchewan, and spent a lot of time on his father's farm in the Qu'Appelle Valley. By his own telling, it was by his mother's efforts more than his own that he ended up at the University of Saskatchewan, in Saskatoon. Once he was there, though, he excelled. Guy studied history and received both a bachelor's and master's degree. It was here that he found the world of words.

Saskatoon has a collegial arts community; at least that's my impression. When I would visit the city, it was common for writers and artists to congregate casually at Lydia's, a local bar and restaurant, every Friday afternoon. And for those who wanted to carry on, there was Buds on Broadway, with live music and dancing. I'm not saying that Guy could always be found at one of these spots, but his generous and friendly nature personify the city for me.

Guy has won the Governor General's Award three times—a remarkable achievement. *Man Descending*, his engaging book of short stories, won in 1982 (it also won the Geoffrey Faber Memorial Prize). *The Englishman's Boy*, the first book in his Western trilogy, won in 1996. His short story collection *Daddy Lenin and Other Stories* won in 2015. **/JH**

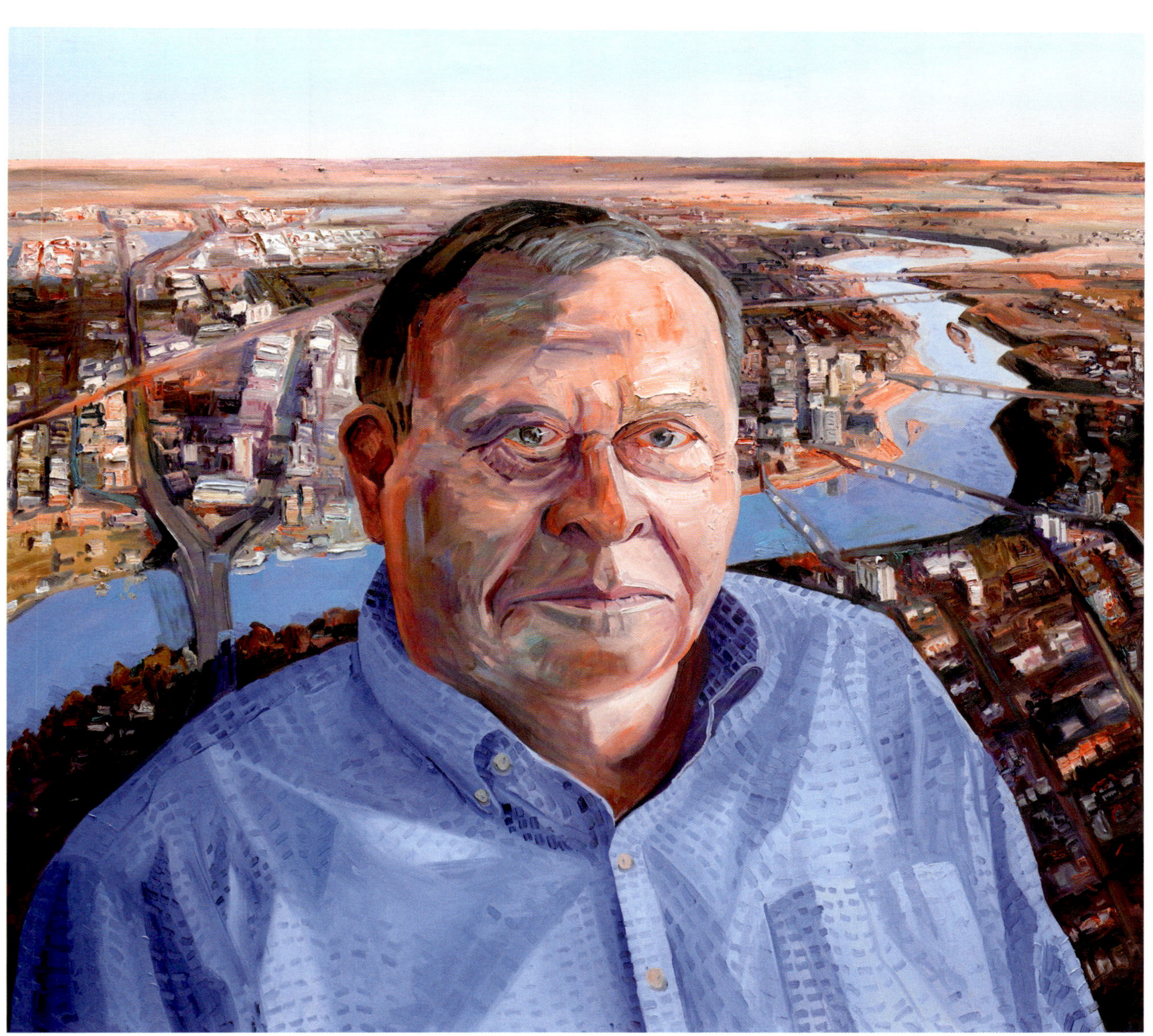

GUY VANDERHAEGHE

The Greeting Card

HAVING TOTTERED INTO my golden years, the sight of my portrait superimposed on an aerial view of Saskatoon leaves me awash in nostalgia. I don't mean naughty *nostalgie de la boue*, but the basted-in-rosy-memory sort that writers are supposed to refrain from. Looking at this painting, I realize I am viewing the background to my writing life.

Fifty years ago, I arrived here, a seventeen-year-old kid from a small Saskatchewan town, for a trial run at the University of Saskatchewan, a run that, given my dismal academic performance in high school, I was certain would prove a headlong sprint to failure. I was only a college student because my mother had discovered that, somehow, I met the bare-minimum requirements for admission at the U of S, and had enrolled me while I was off in B.C. trying to figure out my life. What I thought would be a very short stay turned into a half-century sojourn. My loyalty to the city is due to the fact that the university awoke in me an interest in writing fiction and, later, gave me part-time employment.

I remember wandering the stacks of the old Murray Memorial Library as a freshman, stopping whenever a title caught my eye, and thinking, If I want to, I can read that. I grew up in a place where the school and town libraries were stocked with the sort of books you find at church jumble sales, books that manage to be both excruciatingly life affirming and agonizingly mind deadening. Suddenly, I stumbled on writers who spoke of a world that I had never imagined. With that accident, everything changed for me.

In John Hartman's painting, the university is just out of sight, sitting a little farther back from the second bridge off my left shoulder. But in the picture I carry in my head, it sits squarely in the middle of the city. After all, the university gave a centre to my life, became the hub around which my aspirations began to turn. There I was taught how to *really* read, the first step in becoming a writer.

The South Saskatchewan River has also left its mark on me. It meanderingly bisects the painting. While the river physically divides the city, it also draws it together. On the banks of the Saskatchewan, people come to jog and walk and cycle, or simply to lollygag and soak up sunshine. During my student years, I seldom lived more than a few blocks from this sinuous, beautiful liquid chord that pulses through the city's heart. Walking Saskatoon's bridges, I have seen the river smoke with winter cold and flash scales of eye-aching light under the hot summer sun. I have sat on its brushy east bank, a young man with an old Audubon book in his hand, birds darting and chittering around me. A moment of peace so piercing that now, during sleepless nights, I feel I must have dreamed it.

So, the university and the river. A sappy, nostalgia-drenched greeting card, addressed to me. ■

M.G. VASSANJI ABOVE WOBURN AVENUE

2018 | **oil on linen, 60″ × 66″**

THERE ARE ONLY three authors who have won the Giller Prize twice: Alice Munro, Esi Edugyan, and M.G. Vassanji, who won the inaugural prize in 1994 for *The Book of Secrets*. He won again in 2003 for *The In-Between World of Vikram Lall*. In 2009, his *A Place Within: Rediscovering India* won the Governor General's Award for English-language non-fiction. He is one of our country's most celebrated and critically acclaimed writers.

M.G. is a dedicated traveller, and his initial landscape picks—either Cascais, in Portugal, or Delhi—proved too difficult for me to reach. We finally settled on his neighbourhood in North Toronto, but we were both skeptical. I wondered how I would paint it, and he wondered what he would write about it. We decided to try.

I visited Woburn Avenue in the late fall. The city was grey, but the leaves that remained on the trees were vibrant yellow and orange. This looked promising. The clutter of the Yonge Street shops broke up the grid pattern of local roads. By raising the view point, I was able to see all the way to the waterfront. I thought I had enough to work with, and as the painting developed, I was increasingly happy with it.

I imagined M.G. somewhere in his house, in a small room, on a quiet street, writing all these wonderful books. Creative work can come from unexpected places. **/JH**

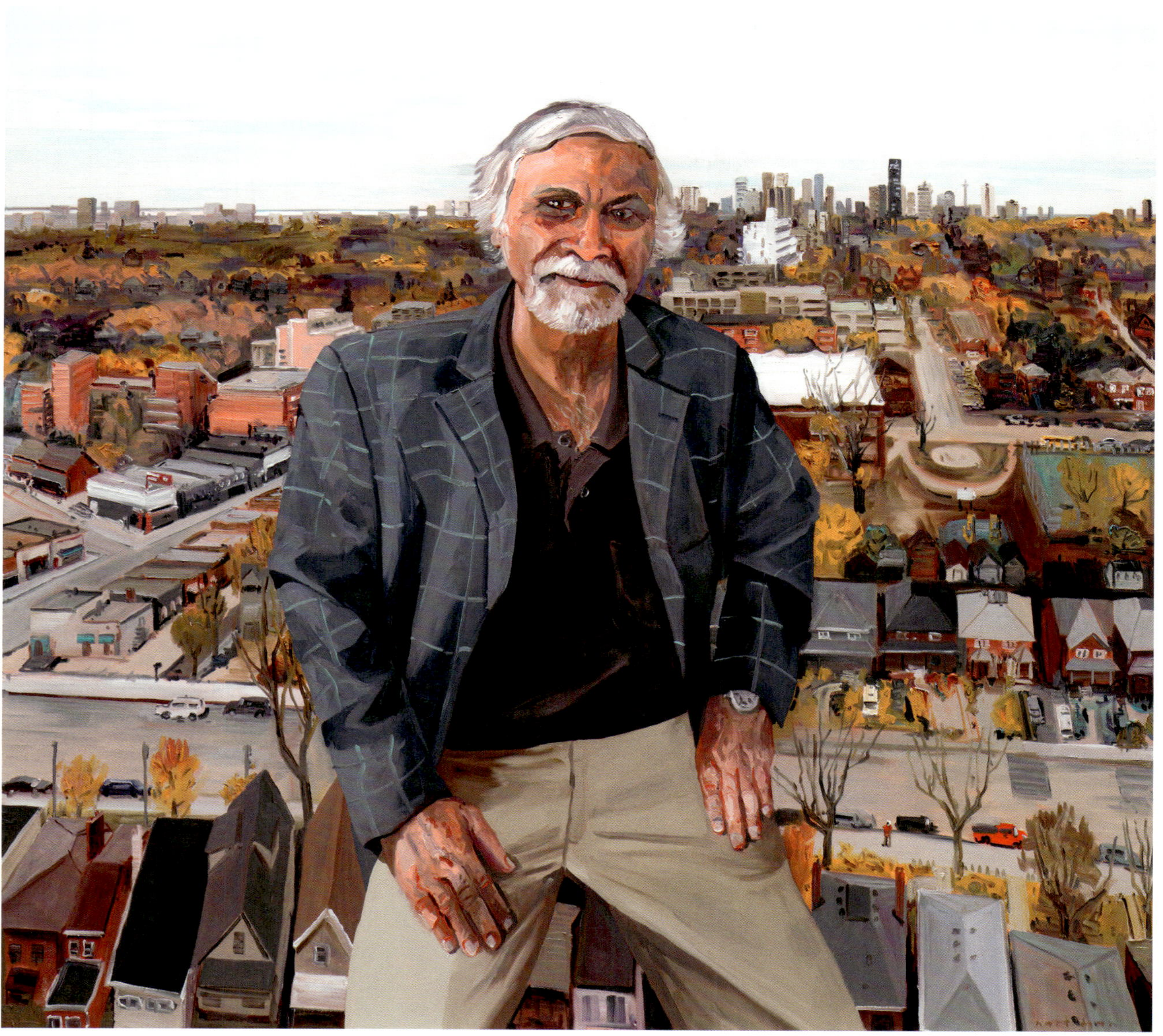

M.G. VASSANJI

The Nomad and the Householder

WHEN A FRIEND URGED, many years ago now, that I only go and look at a few houses with an agent he knew, I resisted. I had never imagined owning a house. There seemed a depressing permanence to the idea. It suggested being stuck, when all my life I had been a nomad—moving from place to place, first from Nairobi to Dar es Salaam as a child, living in a few places before going to Boston, and then four years later to Philadelphia, in each having shifted residences. Ready to go wherever a job called me—even to Timbuktu, I would say—I moved somewhere equally remote: Deep River, Ontario. Two years later, I moved again, to Spadina Avenue, in Toronto.

Except for that stint in Deep River, away from the bustle of Philly and New York and Amtrak stations, I was a city person. I had lived in neighbourhoods where things happened all the time, waking up to the groaning of buses and the clangour of garbage cans, going to sleep lulled by the echoes of police sirens. A house to purchase and live in?

For friendship's sake, we gave Mr. Dutta a chance, and he showed us many places, like a patient salesman, gauging our taste and budget. We knew what kind of house we would purchase if we succumbed: inside the city, traditional red brick and sloping roof, a tree in front, when elsewhere we could afford twice the size with a garage and two or three washrooms, a deck, no trees yet.

We succumbed, and just managed, in the dead of winter, to move from Spadina to Yonge and Lawrence. Suburbia! with a heavy heart. The house had been owned by a single family since the 1920s: Broken shared driveway, broken overgrown backyard—visible once the snow cleared. Inside, all walls covered with thick wallpaper, Victorian style. Ancient fixtures. Dark, dank basement, one wall dedicated to a shelf of forgotten pickle jars. But wonderful flower beds, which bloomed once the snow cleared, and beautiful oak inside. It was an Anglo (for want of a better word) neighbourhood. Bloor and Spadina had its bookstores, cafés, the U of T gym, and the repertoire cinema, which had become a good habit if not exactly a home. At Yonge and Lawrence, we were aliens.

As he grew older, our son attended an all-white school. The European deli gave us a sullen look every time we ventured in. So did the clock-and-watch shop, and the women's boutiques. There were a few hurtful incidents, but let's pretend they did not happen; it's not Canadian to dwell on them. Over the years, the neighbourhood got stirred and mixed; our two kids made friends, went on to other schools and then away. The clock shop and deli and boutiques went their way, too, with their nostalgias of another city. Young families moved in, some of them of African and Asian backgrounds.

No, Yonge and Lawrence has not become like Toronto's Gerrard Street East. We are the familiar old faces on the street now, the couple who like to go out for coffee and apparently don't work. Work? More than ten books got published, produced on an armchair late at night or early in the morning. Travels kept the nomadic heart beating, family brought it home from Nairobi or Dar es Salaam or Delhi or, more recently, Lisbon. It's a good street we moved onto. ■

JOHANNA SKIBSRUD ABOVE ST. JOSEPH DU MOINE

2018 | **oil on linen, 48″ × 54″**

JOHANNA SKIBSRUD WAS thirty when she won the Scotiabank Giller Prize for *The Sentimentalists.* I met her at her farmhouse in St. Joseph du Moine, on Cape Breton Island. I am driving from Chéticamp, just a short distance up the coast, and she is driving from Pictou County on Nova Scotia's North Shore, where she was born and raised. I arrive early, and I wander around the small lake at the back of their property, up the hillside far above their house and down toward the cliffs at the ocean. Johanna arrives with her young daughter and her partner, John Melillo. It has been a long drive for them, but they are gracious.

I first photograph Johanna outside on her small wooden deck. The light is coming upward, reflected from the deck. She looks otherworldly because of the unusual light. We go inside the house, and now we have the right light. I quickly have the photographs I need to paint her portrait.

Months later, back in my studio, I am tempted to paint her in the interior of the house, which is clearly a loved and cared-for space, but the surrounding landscape is so evocative that I chose it instead. **/JH**

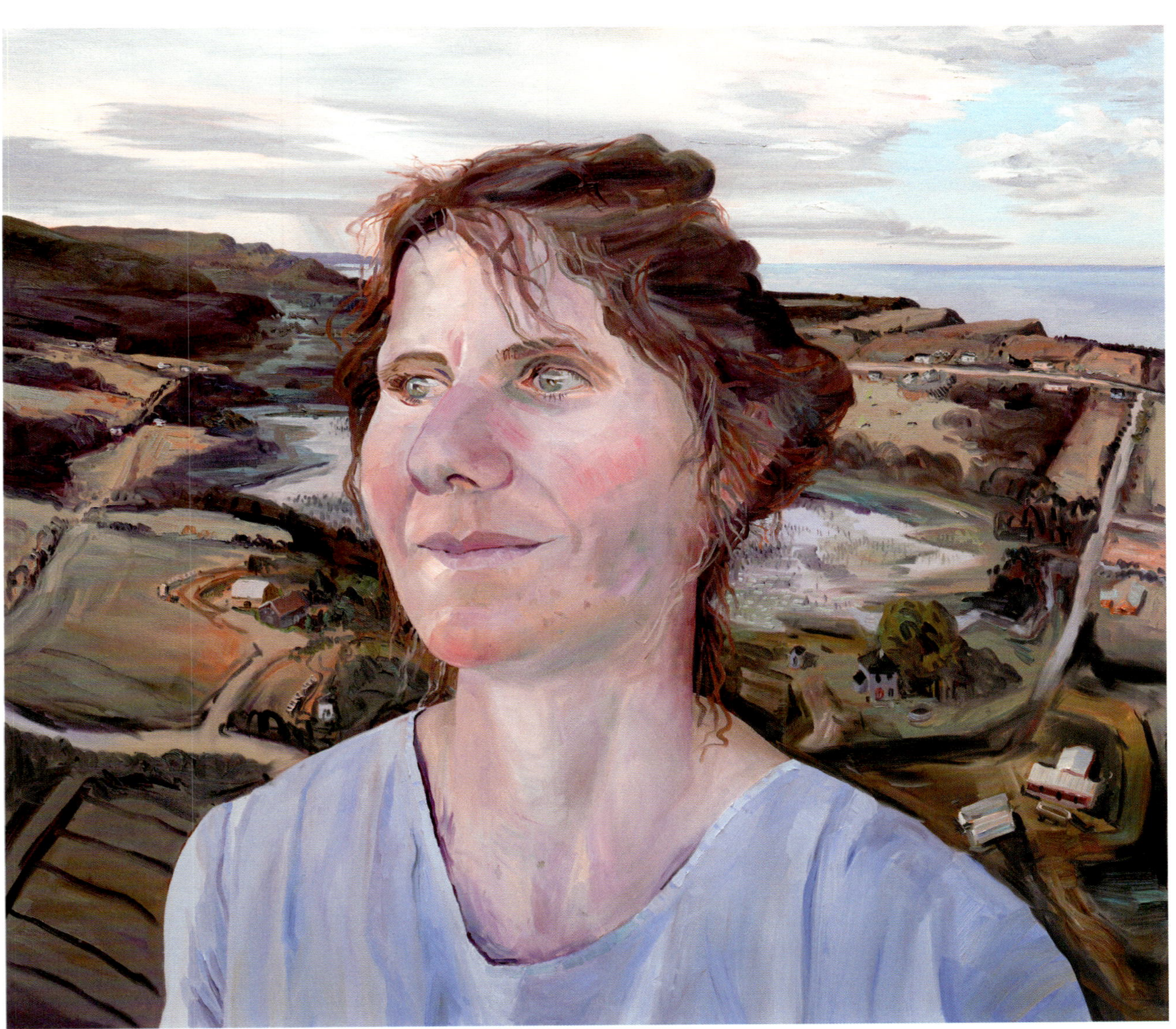

JOHANNA SKIBSRUD

Our Anchor

I CAME BY THE DREAM of transforming a ramshackle farmhouse into a home quite naturally. In the late 1970s, my parents moved from the United States to Pictou County, Nova Scotia, and bought an abandoned farmstead, which today serves as our extended family's anchor and home. For ten years, however—from the time I was one and a half until I was eleven—we lived away, in Kingston, Ontario, and returned to Nova Scotia only in the summertime. Those summers, in my memory, were exquisite, magical times, and despite—or perhaps because of—the time we spent "away," my sister and I inherited my mother's deep longing for the country, and for a particular idea of "home" that she worked hard to instill and provide.

I grew up quite certain that my future would also include a house in the country, and that, someday, I would pass onto my children that same dream, and experience, of "home." But many years later, when several good friends of mine began moving back to the East Coast and living out their own versions of that dream, I was momentarily distracted. I'd recently embraced my love of big cities, was living in Paris, and had fallen in love with a man who couldn't imagine living outside of New York.

A few years after that, while visiting one of my oldest friends in St. Joseph du Moine, Cape Breton, she mentioned that the place next

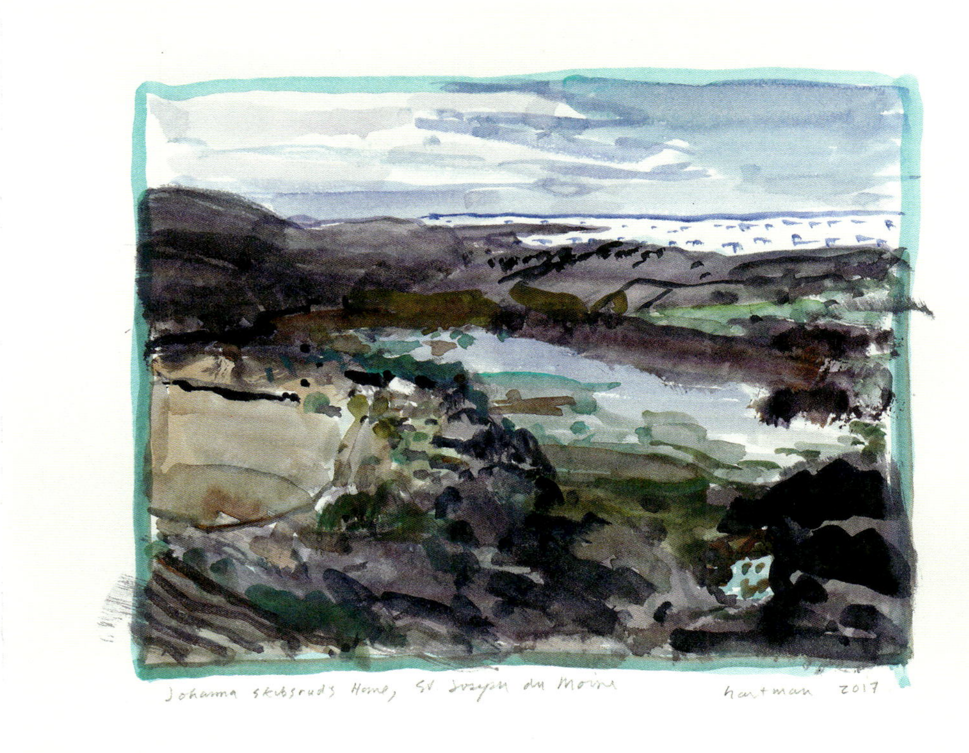

Johanna Skibsrud's Home, St. Joseph du Moine 2017
watercolour on paper
9″ × 11.25″

door to hers was for sale. We wandered down the hill to the boarded-up place, which hadn't been lived in for years, then down across the lawn—beneath the tallest poplars I'd ever seen—to the stream. When I turned around and looked back at the house, I had a feeling people talk about, but that I'd rarely experienced. *I just knew:* this was home.

My husband and I return to St. Joseph du Moine every summer now, and each year we fall more deeply in love with the place. We love the lake that borders our property—where the water starts out high every May then gradually recedes, becoming a haven for ducks and herons and a single bald eagle who, like us, returns every year.

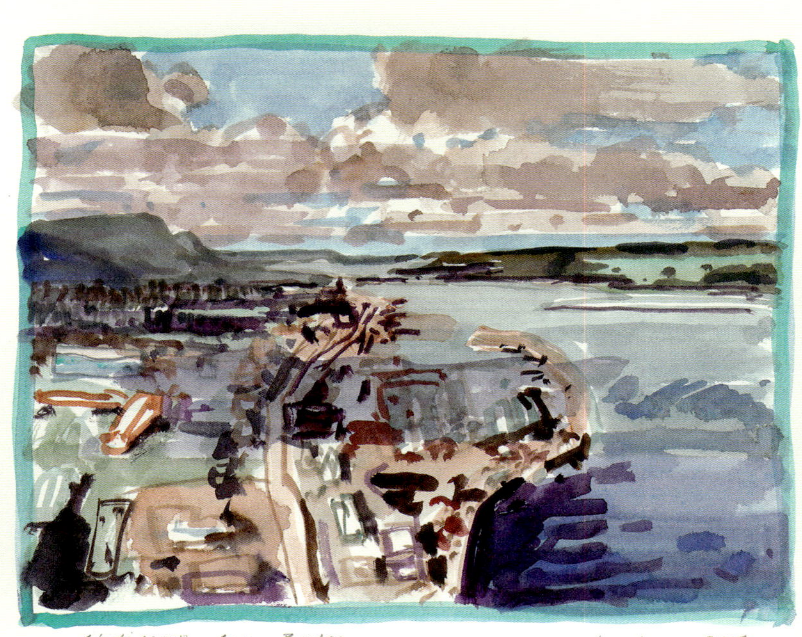

Cheticamp, Cape Breton 2017
watercolour on paper
9″ × 11.25″

We love the local beaches—some of the most beautiful I've ever seen—where we collect beach glass and speckled rocks and, once, dug from the sand the entire vertebrae of a right whale. We love the woods and fields around the house, where the passage of the season can be gauged by the wildflowers and summer berries currently in bloom. We even love the changeable and not always favourable weather: the fog in the mornings, the torrential rainstorms, and the suete winds that sometimes shake our old house at its root. We love that our daughter—now just four—loves the place as much as we do, or perhaps more. She was only six weeks old when we took her to the house for the first time, and it is one of the great joys of my life to see the way that her own memories, and sense of place and home, are being shaped by it.

It amazes me to think about the way that a pattern of a life is constructed just like the mysterious marks the ocean makes in the sand, or the layers of rock in the cliff: one element or form leading to, blurring into, and becoming the next. Without knowledge or forethought, but nevertheless with absolute certainty, trust, and direction. ■

SARA TILLEY, ELLISTON

2017 | **oil on linen, 48″ × 54″**

THE TILLEY SIDE of Sara's family come from Elliston, on the east side of the tip of the Bonavista Peninsula, which separates Bonavista Bay and Trinity Bay, on the east coast of Newfoundland. This stretch of shoreline is defined by rocky cliffs, eroded by the constant pounding of the North Atlantic.

Elliston, known as the Root Cellar Capital of the World, is the town nestled on the far shore of the bay behind Sara's head. Immediately behind her is Elliston Point, currently home to a puffin colony. At the base of the bay, separating the point and the town, is a glorious, sweeping pebble beach.

Sara's novel *Duke*, which won the 2015 Winterset Award, is partly set in Elliston. In St. John's, she may be best known as an actor and a playwright, as well as a novelist. **/JH**

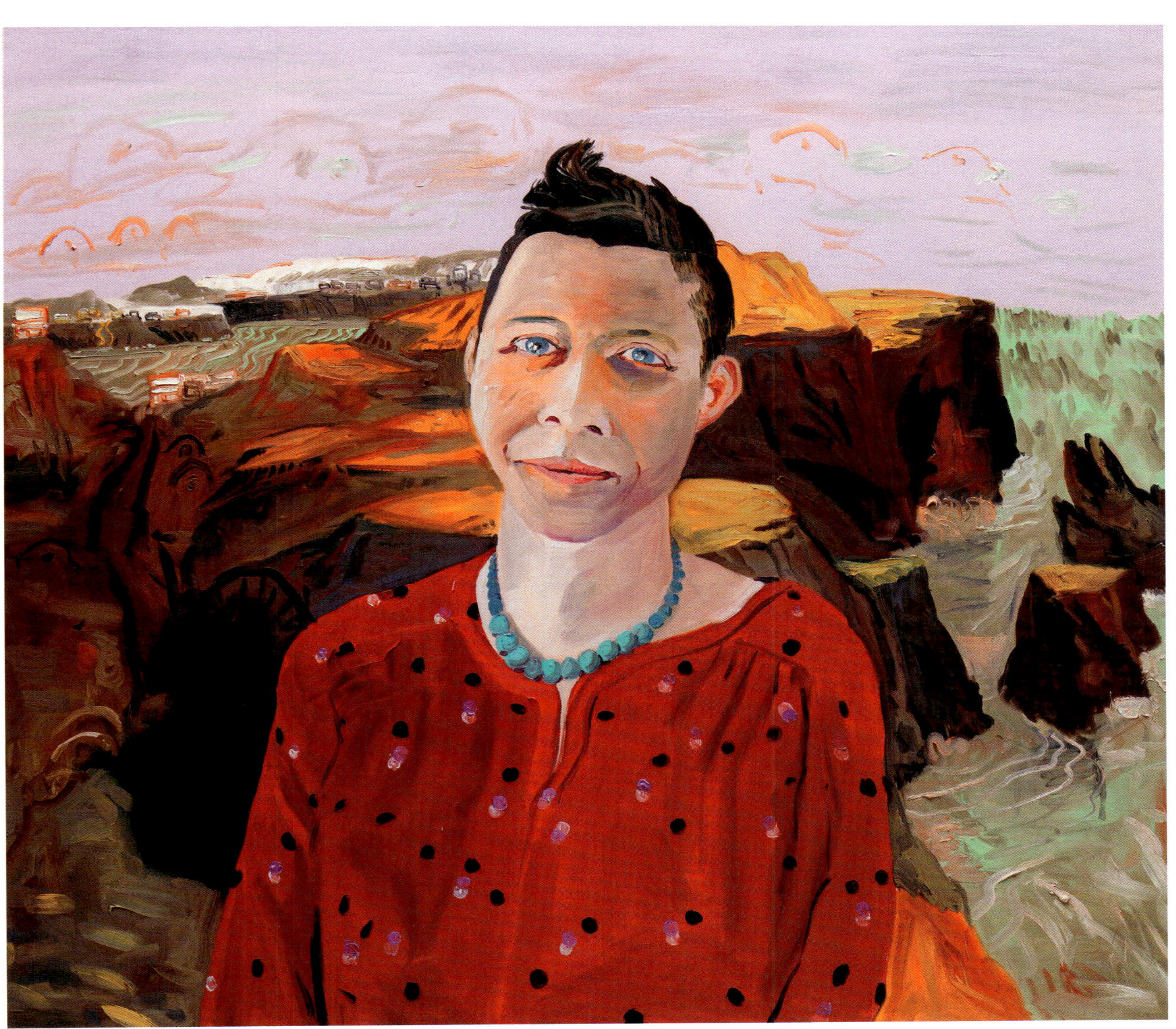

SARA TILLEY

An Othered Life

JOHN HARTMAN HAS depicted me within the geography of my novel *Duke*. While much of the book takes place in Alaska, its home is Elliston, on Trinity Bay, Newfoundland and Labrador, where the Tilley family were merchants before there was an "e" in our name—the signage arrived spelled incorrectly, and the Till(e)ys adapted accordingly. The Elliston store/post office/family home was the literal beginning place for my novel, as it is where my father and I, in 2004, discovered stacks of letters and logbooks belonging to my great-grandfather Duke Tilly. They'd been hidden in a cupboard upstairs, and until then Dad had neglected his crowbar. The documents became my source material.

Elliston was mysterious—too far from town for us to go often, though we memorably stayed there in sleeping bags on the floor to see Queen Elizabeth greet a replica of *The Matthew*, which an actor dressed as Giovanni Caboto sailed into Bonavista once. It was my first experience of both royalty and protestors—a group of Indigenous people affronted by the colonial pageant. I told my brother we were "indoor camping." Even if there *were* ghosts in the huge, empty house, they were related to us.

Once called Bird Island Cove, Elliston used to be a major community, connecting sealers and fisherman with merchants like the Tillys and Templemans, who bought their catch and sold them back their necessities. In recent years, the town has become known for its Puffin Festival, its claim to Root Cellar Capital of the World, its sealers museum, and for its food and culture festival—Roots, Rants, and Roars—where chefs concoct nouvelle scoffs on the beach my ancestors once owned. It's a sandy one, complete with a perfect, tiny takeout, where, in a post–Puffin Fest lineup, I once heard someone describe his "usual"—two cheeseburgers and a chaser of prune juice, "for the man I'll be tomorrow." The takeout actually stocked prune juice for this fella, because that's how small Elliston is. Still, you'd be hard-pressed for a camping spot in September on account of the foodie influx, all seeking a heady encounter with bakeapple foam and turr tartare.

The Tilley House, while restored on the exterior and given heritage designation when I was a kid, has fallen victim to vandalism and years of disuse. The front steps have rotted away, the clapboard is weeping rust, and most of the windows have been boarded over. The inside, though, is still as strong and true as ever. Good bones. Architects have admired it and quoted figures needed to restore it, and my father has dreamed about ways to revive the family store as a museum or an artist residency or offices—anything but wasted space. This is seemingly impossible without patrons, partnerships, or other methods beyond his grasp. If I were another kind of person, maybe I could see a way to save it.

Instead, the thought paralyzes me. I have no real resources except my creativity, and I've used that as well as I can to make a second house, a second store, a second Elliston home that will never rot and crumble. Like the characters who live there, my Elliston only somewhat resembles the reality that inspired it. I suppose I can sit with that guilt a while yet—of writing fiction inspired by family, trying on their skeletons and making them other. An othered life is better than disappearing, right? These are the lies I tell myself. ■

DAVID ADAMS RICHARDS ABOVE THE BARTIBOG AND MIRAMICHI RIVERS

2018 | **oil on linen, 66″ × 60″**

DAVID ADAMS RICHARDS suggested I read René Girard's book *I See Satan Fall Like Lightning* before I painted his portrait. He wanted me to understand Girard's thoughts on predestination and free will, ideas that go back to Saint Augustine. They certainly are central to David's writing, which locates itself among the lives of the working-class people of the Miramichi. By my count, David has written sixteen novels about them.

As I approached Newcastle, New Brunswick, coming to visit David, a lightning storm swept over the town from the south and blackened the sky. It felt Biblical.

David has won the Governor General's Award for both fiction and non-fiction: *Nights Below Station Street*, a novel, in 1988, and *Lines on the Water: A Fisherman's Life on the Miramichi* in 1998. In 2000, he was co-winner of the Giller Prize for *Mercy among the Children*. In 2017, shortly after I visited him, he was appointed to the Senate of Canada.

I painted David above a stretch of the Miramichi, from the mouth of the Bartibog River to Newcastle. This is home for him and his wife, Peggy, and the home of his fiction, although he argues that the true home of his fiction is in his characters. Peggy's family place is in the lower right corner. In the lower left, hovering between David and the Sts. Peter and Paul Church, are a Miramichi salmon, Saint Augustine, and Job sitting on the dung heap. In the upper right, above the back country of the Bartibog, Satan falls from the sky and Adam and Eve are expelled from the Garden of Eden. But the thunderstorm has cleared, and fine weather approaches from the west. **/JH**

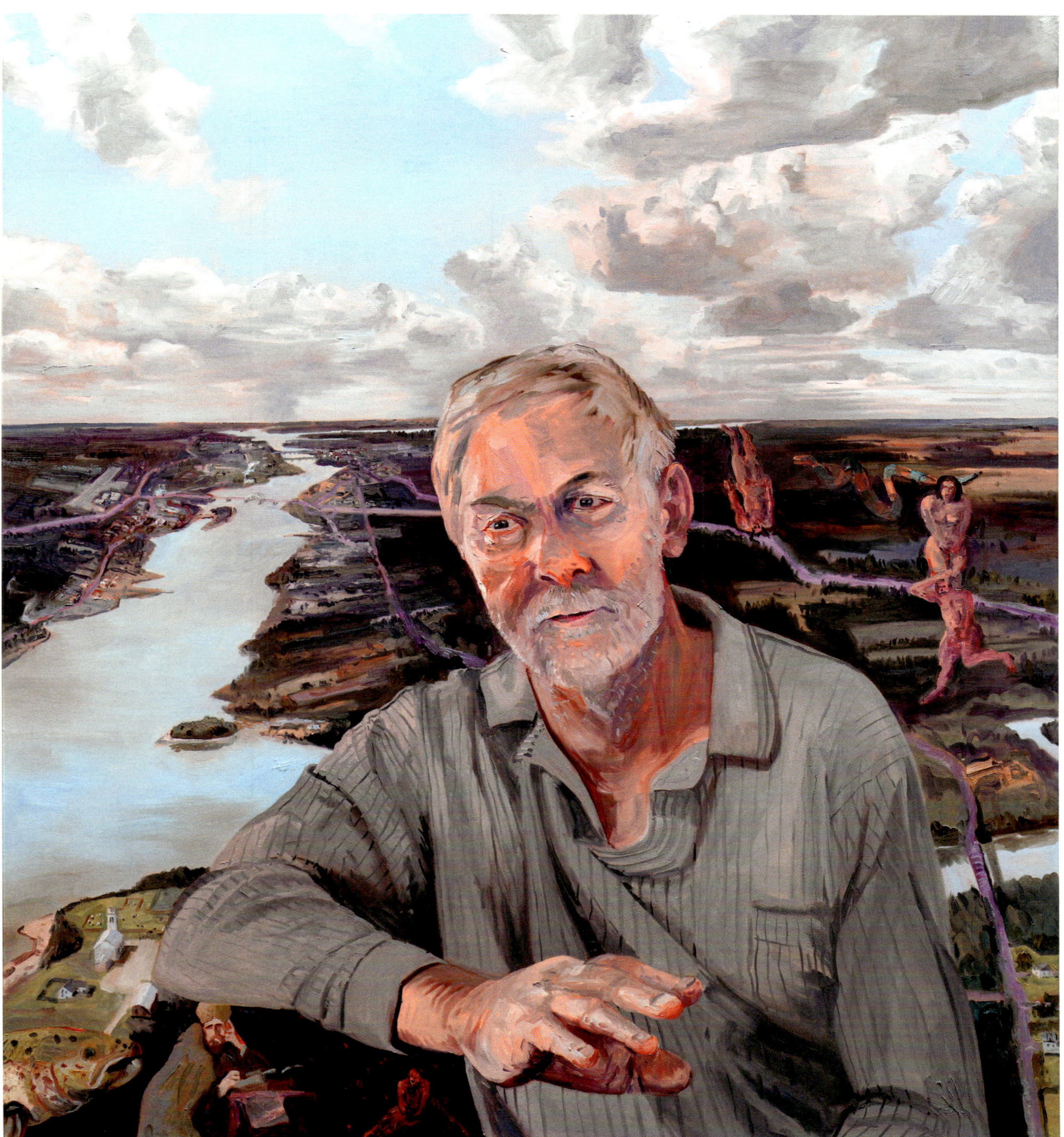

DAVID ADAMS RICHARDS

Dimensions True

THE MIRAMICHI IS a great river, with a myriad of tributaries, branches, and streams, covering half of my province, flowing from just north of our capital out to the Northumberland Strait and Gulf of Saint Lawrence. It is the setting for most, but not all of my work. The human heart—the spirit of humanity—is infused in all of it. This is my river and the people in it—their courage, grace, and pride, their tremendous nobility, whether poor or rich—have been my inspiration.

I have written about these people, the people who are part of this river, my entire life. My canon is, in one way or the other, a tribute to and a telling of them. They are part of the land, and the land is infused in them, just as the land of the steppe is in the soul of Gorky or Tolstoy. As one of my characters in *Crimes against My Brother* says, "Human drama, and human greatness, unfolds wherever humans are."

I have written about the human drama that occurs on my great river, and you can see a part of it in this painting. The closer you look, the more you may realize: Sts. Peter and Paul Church, where my wife and I were married; the great Bartibog flowing into the Miramichi, where seven of my books are centred; the road where my wife was born; the idea of faith and hope in the figure of Saint Augustine; and all evil intent, as in the form of Satan finally falling through the night.

I have hunted and fished on the very tributary one sees here, have taken salmon and trout from the river, and moose and deer in the autumn of the year. The woods moved toward the northwest, where friends of mine have spent their lives hunting and trapping, and where the Miramichi itself spreads away to the towns and industry in the distance, where I have lived and created most of my life.

The true dimension of my novels is the human spirit, the courage and greatness of sacrifice and the human soul on this Grand River. The characters are the men and women of my blood, and I write about the unending moments of tragedy, magnanimity, and truth that unfold there. If you read about Ivan Basterache in *Evening Snow Will Bring Such Peace* or about Autumn and Percy in *Mercy among the Children*, you will have a sense of why I love them and what the river and the bay mean to them and to their humanity. The greatest realization is that these Miramichi characters, in all their humanity, flaws, and goodness, are you and me. ■

GEORGE BOWERING ABOVE OLIVER

2018 | **oil on linen, 60″ × 66″**

I FIND IT hard to imagine George Bowering as Canada's first Parliamentary Poet Laureate. The title sounds so serious, and George loves to clown around. He kept making faces while I photographed him in his Vancouver apartment. Finally, after about ten minutes, he stopped and I began to get some useful photos. Despite his pranks, he made my job very easy: in 2015, George published *Writing the Okanagan*, selections from over forty books of poetry, fiction, and history about the valley, mostly about the town of Lawrence, his fictional version of his hometown, Oliver. I brought the book with me as I walked the hills above the high school in Oliver, went down to the lake to see if the diving platform was still moored off the shore, and scrambled up the mountainsides to the east and west to get the full view of the river and the town.

George has published over 120 books: plays, memoirs, chapbooks, literacy criticism, poetry, short fiction, and fiction. He is one of only four authors (along with Margaret Atwood, Douglas LePan, and Michael Ondaatje) who have won an English-language Governor General's Award for both fiction and poetry, for the novel *Burning Water* in 1980 and the books *Rocky Mountain Foot* and *The Gangs of Kosmos* in 1969.

I have painted George above Oliver. On the right are the low hills on the west side of town where he would scramble up after (or instead of going to) school. Behind his head is the home where his sister lived. On the left, the Okanagan River runs its course down the valley, after leaving the lake where George and his friends would swim to wash off the dust of a day's work in the Okanagan orchards. **/JH**

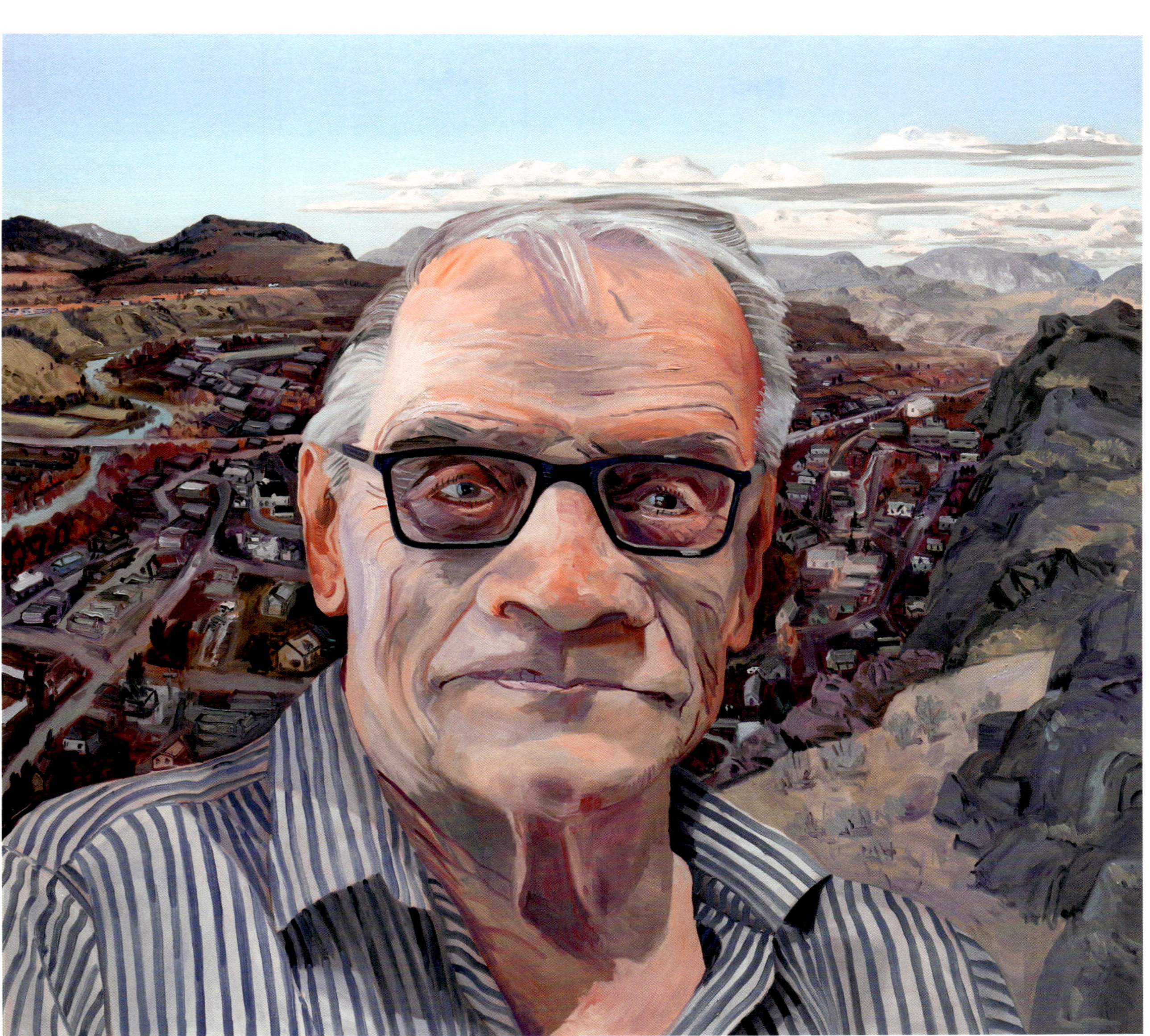

GEORGE BOWERING

Next Best

WHEN WE WENT DOWN to the Oliver Theatre on a Saturday afternoon to see a western in colour, we saw the same landscape we would see the next day, when we went for a hike in the hills on either side of the Okanagan Valley. We were careful about where we put a foot down, because of cactuses, because of rattlesnakes, because of animal poop that hadn't baked yet. A semi-arid climate, we were told in school: Yet there were wet slugs in the long grass around the cherry tree trunks. There were pheasants with eggs or chicks in that long grass, too, and our young hearts would just about stop for the sudden noise when those big birds took to the treetops.

The shade of the trees made wonderful respite when the sun's blaze went to three figures Fahrenheit. We boys took our shirts off when school let us out in late June, and we didn't put them back on till they made us return in September. Nobody's house or car had air conditioning, and neither did the stores and pool halls on the main drag, also known as Highway 97. It rained hard one July day every year, just in time to ruin the cherry crop, and again on a Sunday in September, so a guy could sleep in instead of picking apples all day.

I left the valley at seventeen to go to college near the ocean. That's when I started wearing pyjamas at night—the bed felt cold and damp. That's when I started falling asleep in class, because of all that air pressure at sea level. That's where I saw people paying money for apples, and I thought that was like paying money for stones or animal poop. Later I found out that those things happen too. You pay a price for living where God and humans settle for next best.

Yes, eventually I settled for next best too. I have been living in cities for sixty-five years, some of them on other continents, but I continue driving up to the South Okanagan a couple of times a year. When I catch my first glimpse of dry hills and rock slides, I think, This is where God said, "I finally got it right."

Still, for the usual reasons, the valley has become less of a paradise over time, just as my body has descended on the scale from Adonis-like to visibly mortal. Most of the fruit trees have given way to the more fashionable and remunerative grape vines. In one awful year, my mother, my sister, and my kid brother all died and left only our younger brother in that warm desert air.

But the sagebrush and cactuses and rattlesnakes are still in those hills and some of the backyards, and later this week I will be there again too. ■

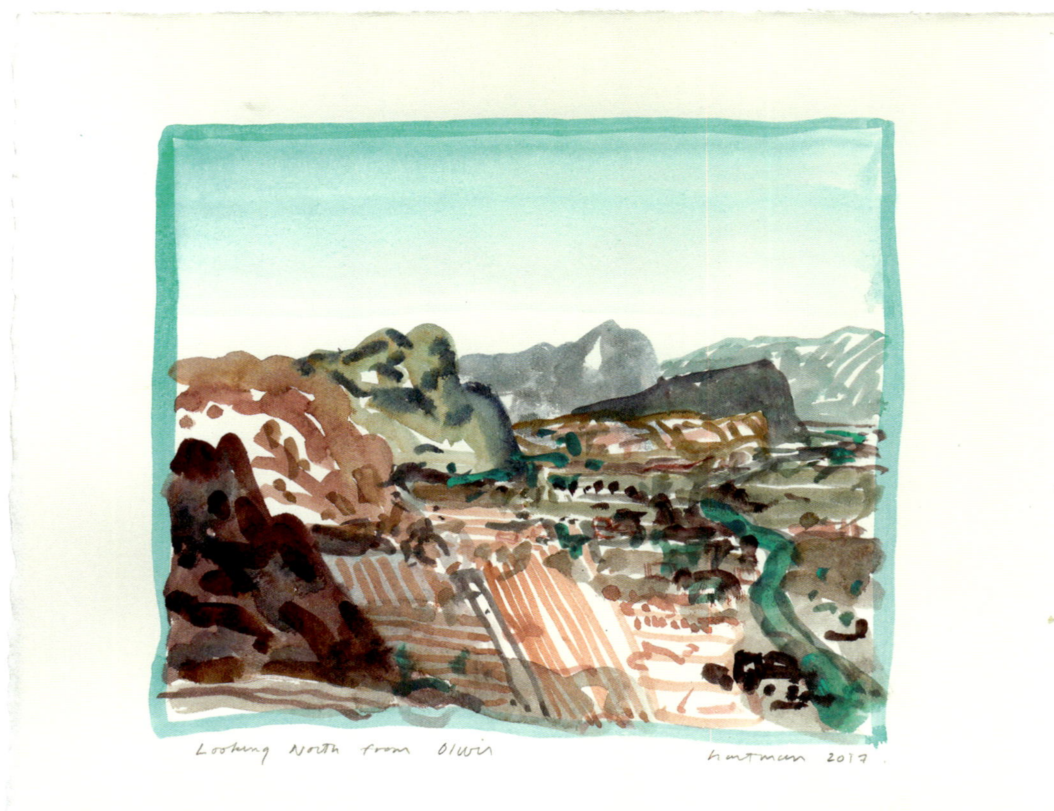

Looking North from Oliver 2017
watercolour on paper
9.25" × 11.25"

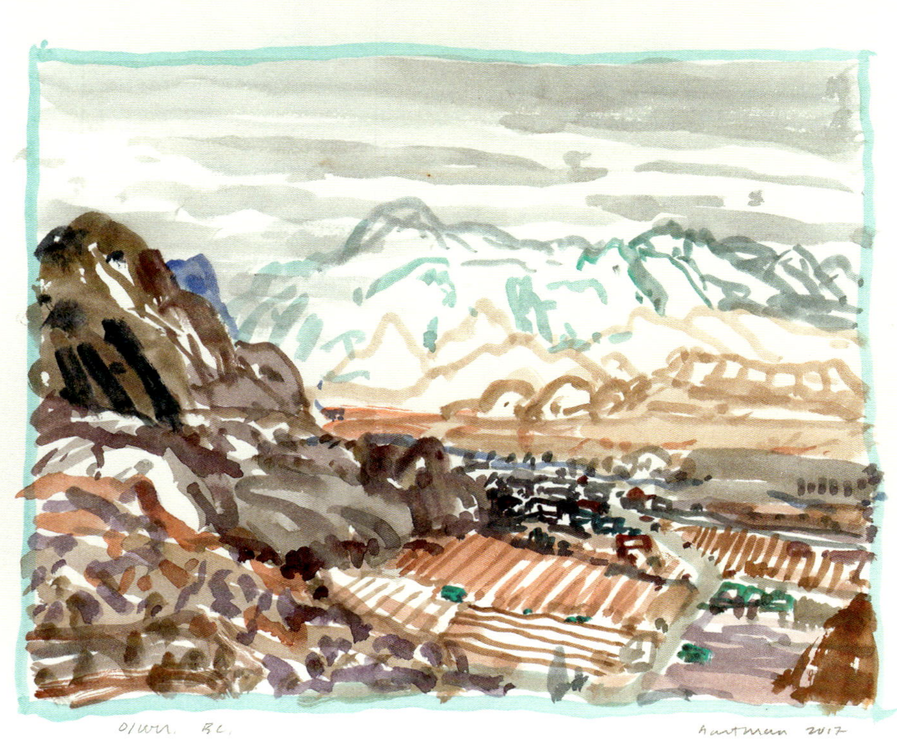

Oliver, BC 2017
watercolour on paper
9″ × 11.25″

CAMILLA GIBB ABOVE KENSINGTON MARKET

2018 | **oil on linen, 60″ × 66″**

I PAINTED CAMILLA GIBB above Kensington Market, in Toronto. When you look past her and down at the foreground, you see the roof of a parking garage, close to the corner of Baldwin Street and Augusta Avenue, at the heart of the market. On the left of the canvas, you look up past Spadina Avenue toward the towers of Bay Street; on the right side, you look toward the CN Tower.

When I met Camilla, we discussed living in the countryside. She seemed to be considering a move to the area where I live. She even had a property in mind. Yet she clearly loved her part of the city—the gritty, ever-changing, congested, wonderful conglomeration of food shops, clothing stores, bars, and restaurants that make up Kensington Market. Camilla has a PhD in social anthropology, from the University of Oxford, and was an academic until she began pursuing full-time writing in 2000. She reinvented her life and became an award-winning author, just like the market she lives beside reinvents itself with each new generation. **/JH**

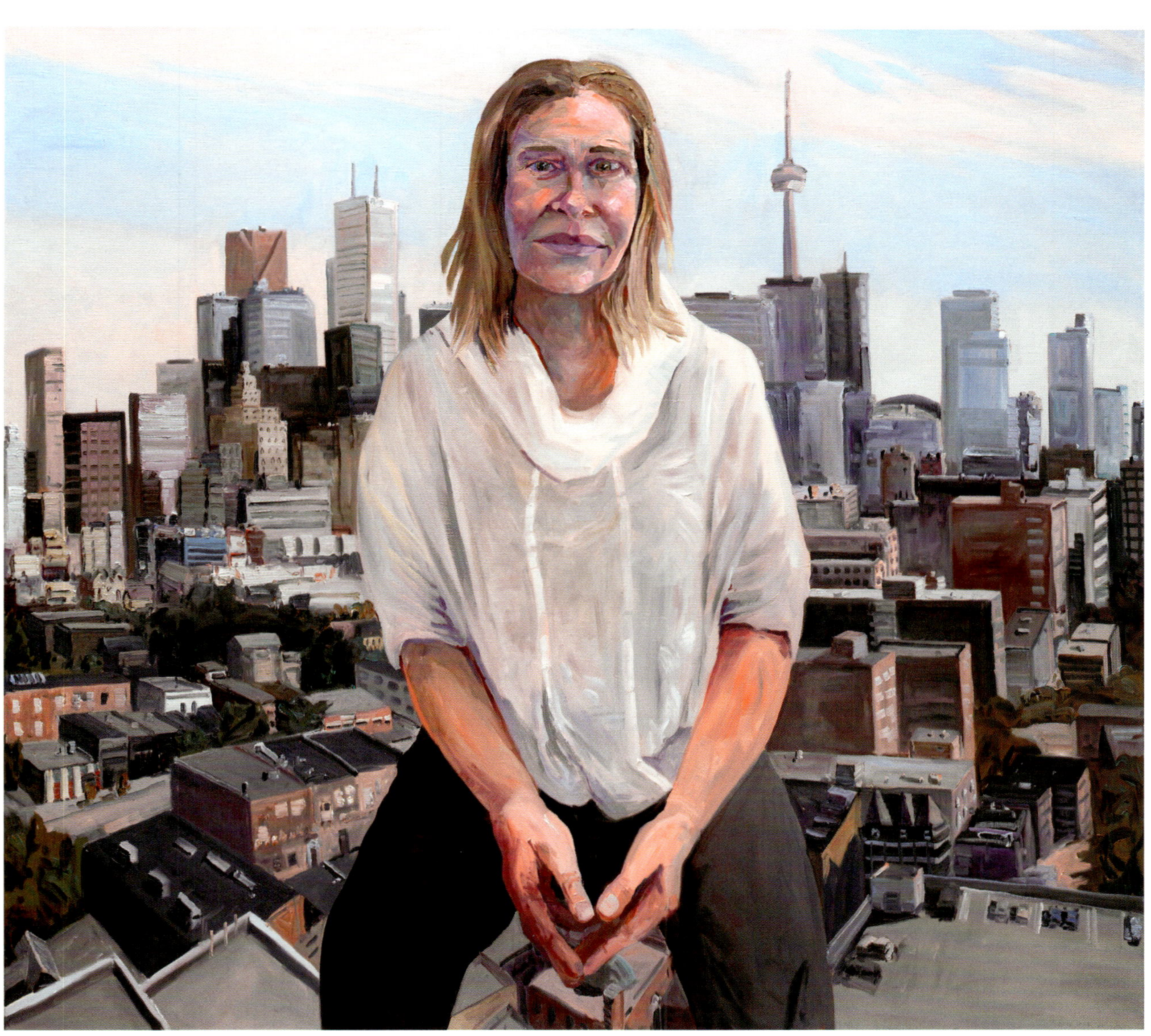

CAMILLA GIBB

Dynamic Heart

WHEN I WAS A CHILD, my father had a girlfriend who was far too young for him but just young enough for me. She was more of a big sister than a mother figure. She would take me on urban adventures, most of them centred around food, in large part because my father had very rigid ideas about eating: two meals a day, no snacking, no sugar. My more-like-a-big-sister and I went out and ate on the days I was staying at my father's. We made sure to leave enough time to work up an appetite before dinner so that he never knew what we'd been up to.

Our conspiracy often led us across the city to Kensington Market, a place I considered and still consider the heart of Toronto. We would sample unfamiliar cheeses at Global Cheese on Kensington Avenue before ordering the same extra-old English cheddar that my father liked. We would taste different salamis and chorizos and buy dried apricots and almonds from the bins in front of the stores along Baldwin Street. A guy with a stand on wheels would sell us hot cashews. We would visit the fishmongers and stare into the tanks, and cluck at the chickens in their cages in front of the kosher poultry place on Augusta. I was fond of buying a chicken foot for five cents, and would amuse myself by pulling at the exposed tendons to form and release its claws.

I never imagined I would grow up to live on the market's fringes; I never imagined I would grow up at all. But here I am, forty years later, introducing my own daughter to its institutions and new arrivals. Here we eat churros and empanadas, buy fruit and bread, and pump up our bike tires. On the way home, I can't help pointing out the tattoo shop my brother owned for fifteen years. ("I *know*, Mama, you've told me like a hundred times.") I try not to bore her with more stories of how it used to be.

Much has been written about the market's multicultural history, most recently in the form of a lament for what was. As a dynamic microcosm of Toronto, the threat of and resistance to local gentrification reflect tensions in the city's evolution as a whole. While towers rise up on all sides, the market remains a provocative place, one of incubation and experimentation. There is a metaphor here about the need to protect a space for defiance and innovation, whether in entrepreneurialism or art, in the face of one's own gentrification. Perhaps, in mid-life, I live in close proximity to Kensington Market as a reminder to myself. ■

DAVID BERGEN ABOVE THE RAT AND RED RIVERS

2018 | **oil on linen, 60″ × 66″**

WHEN I STEPPED out of my car at the junction of the Red River and the Rat River, my boot came up with two inches of glue-like black dirt. I finally understood what "black gumbo soil" meant. I was here on David Bergen's instruction to scout the landscape for his portrait. I photographed and sketched the river, along with the flat, rich farmland surrounding it. I stood on the site where the SS *International,* a paddlewheeler, dropped off the first contingent of Mennonite settlers on August 1, 1874. I talked with David's childhood friend Dave Neufeld, who welded together the steel barrels that floated their raft downriver to Winnipeg. I was reading David's award-winning first novel, *A Year of Lesser*, so I had lunch in Niverville, the hometown he had fictionalized. I imagined the novel's characters walking the streets.

David is a man of focus. In his house in Winnipeg, he told me that he wrote *A Year of Lesser* on his lunch breaks, while teaching high school English. He is tall and lanky, and I wanted to capture his full figure, so I painted him sitting on a chair. Then I removed the chair, so he is floating above the landscape of his childhood. **/JH**

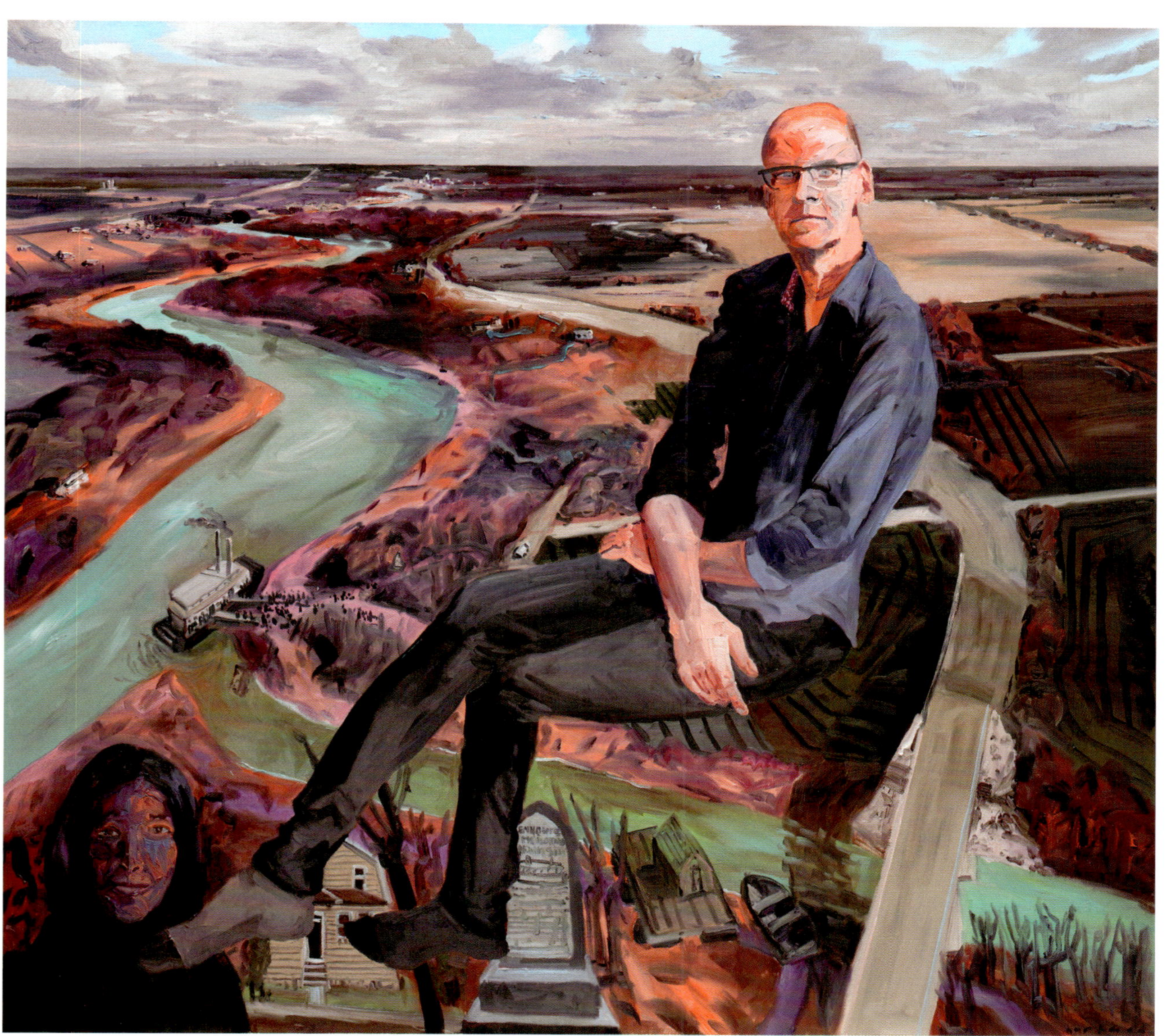

DAVID BERGEN

Mrs. Dyck

MY LIFE HAS CONSISTED of two belief systems: religious faith and poetic faith. As a youth, I had to memorize Bible passages. A line from 1 Corinthians 13 still bounces around in my head: "When I was a child, I spake as a child, I understood as a child, I thought as a child: but when I became a man, I put away childish things." As an adult, I threw off the yoke of religious faith and fell in with fiction. This was not a big leap, for both faiths deal in the currency of the word.

I spent my formative years in a small town called Niverville, Manitoba. With my first novel, *A Year of Lesser*, I offered a place called Lesser, which was a fictional map laid over the town of my youth. Recently, I drove the 311 west through Niverville. Here was the Richert farm, there Excel Feed Services, where I worked one cold and long and lonely winter as a truck driver and wrote my first stories. Here was Wm. Dyck & Sons, where I operated a forklift, there the Mennonite Brethren Church in which I was baptized—the same church with the blue rug where I baptized one of my characters. Here was the arena where I scored my first goal, and there the high school where I studied Maugham and Conrad and Twain—all taught by Helene Dyck, whom I secretly loved and who allowed four of her grade eleven students to build a raft and float down the Red River and report about it rather than write an essay on Huck Finn.

We built our raft out of four forty-five-gallon drums that we welded to a metal frame, and onto this frame we bolted two-by-sixes. We launched it at the junction of the Red and the Rat, and we floated down the Red for two days and a night, ending up at the locks of the floodway, more than seventy kilometres downriver. It was late October and at night there was frost, and so we built a fire on the raft, in a metal drum, and sang and drank and smoked cigarillos. Life stretched out before me.

Mrs. Dyck wore her long hair parted in the middle and loved the two Joans—Baez and Didion. I was not dissuaded by the fact that she was six years older than me and was married to a farmer with lots of money. All I could imagine was that a farmer would have no idea who Didion was. Mrs. Dyck wrote me a letter after I published my first book, and said that she did not recognize the student who had become the writer. She was very surprised and very pleased, as if to say, Look at what has come out of Niverville.

This was a town governed by a religious rigour that was consuming and hypocritical and pious. Beneath the piety roiled a conflict of desires—sexual, mercantile, heavenly. And I was part of the mess. And then, happily, I found a new shape—fiction—which required once again, as all faiths do, that willing suspension of disbelief for the moment. ■

LISA MOORE
ABOVE BROAD COVE

2017 | **oil on linen, 60″ × 66″**

THIS IS BROAD COVE, on the western shore of Conception Bay, in Newfoundland. You are looking southwest from above it. Lisa Moore has family here, her husband's family. Her sister-in-law runs the general store on the highway at the south end of town, in the upper left of the painting. Lisa's sister also has a house nearby.

When I arrived in Broad Cove, the sun was shining. I had three places to locate and sketch: Lisa's house; a pond about three kilometres inland, on which Lisa has a remote cabin; and a waterfall on the river that runs from the pond to the sea. I also needed to sketch the community as a whole. I love this process of figuring out the configuration of the land, the water, the buildings, the roads, and the bridges that make a place *lived in*.

Lisa's home is among the group of houses on the right side of the painting, where the river empties into the base of the cove. The cabin is on the distant pond near the upper right horizon, and the waterfall is just a short distance down the river, flowing from the pond to the sea.

Lisa was born in St. John's, where she now lives. She studied at the Nova Scotia College of Art and Design and intended to become a visual artist. Instead, she became a celebrated writer. Her second book, *Open*, was a commercial and critical success, and her following book, *Alligator*, won a Commonwealth Writers' Prize. Her novel *February* landed on the Man Booker Prize longlist and won Canada Reads in 2013. **/JH**

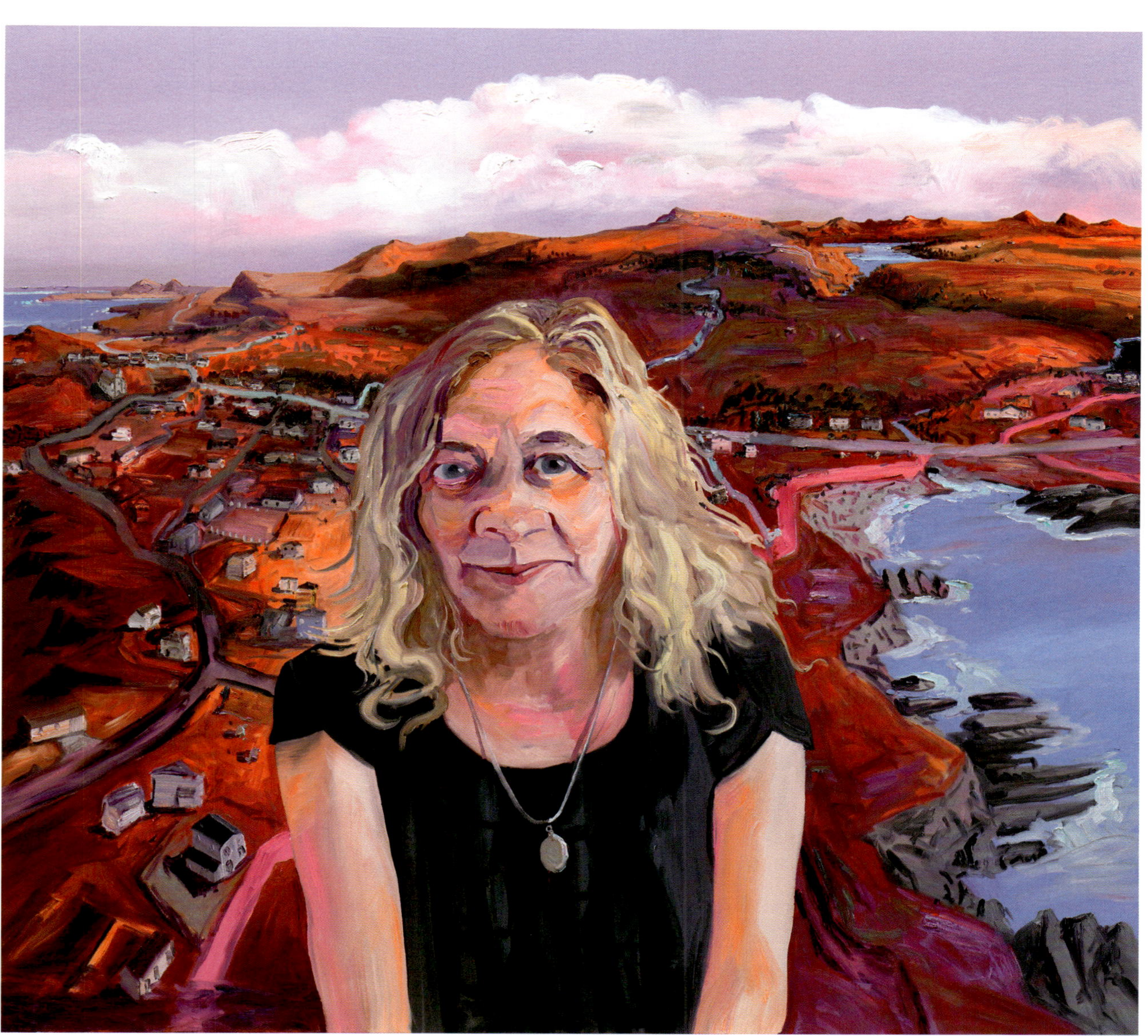

LISA MOORE

Bubbles

MY FATHER-IN-LAW'S birthday party, and I have a bubble wand for the children.

A chartreuse tube of transparent plastic, shaped like a sword, full of bubble potion. I draw out the wand, a wide oval flicks open, and a stretch of clear soap, iridescent—my face reflected on the bubble's delicate rainbow skin. It's trembling, tearing away, tottering off the wand.

The first bubble floats up, dipping close to the lawn, green blades threatening to pierce it, and up again, out over the river, beyond to the dead yellow grass of the Heart's Content Barrens, where we can hear the singing of the lost souls who died in a snowstorm a century ago.

Each bubble holds a world, a different me.

The moose coalesces in the dark, stinking of peat and moss and wet bark. It's a galaxy of burnt-out stars, black. It was always there.

I don't hit it; I drive through it. A grafting of flesh, all the parts of my Yaris fly up, suspended for seconds, maybe hours or years, in the sky, the windshield intact, but a spiderweb of silvered cracks spreads over it with dazzling speed.

When I touch the brakes nothing happens. The car is released from my will. I feel the moose draw a breath, an exhale full of solemnity and clotted mucus. I feel a chrysanthemum of heat, tensile whiskers on my cheek. The last thing.

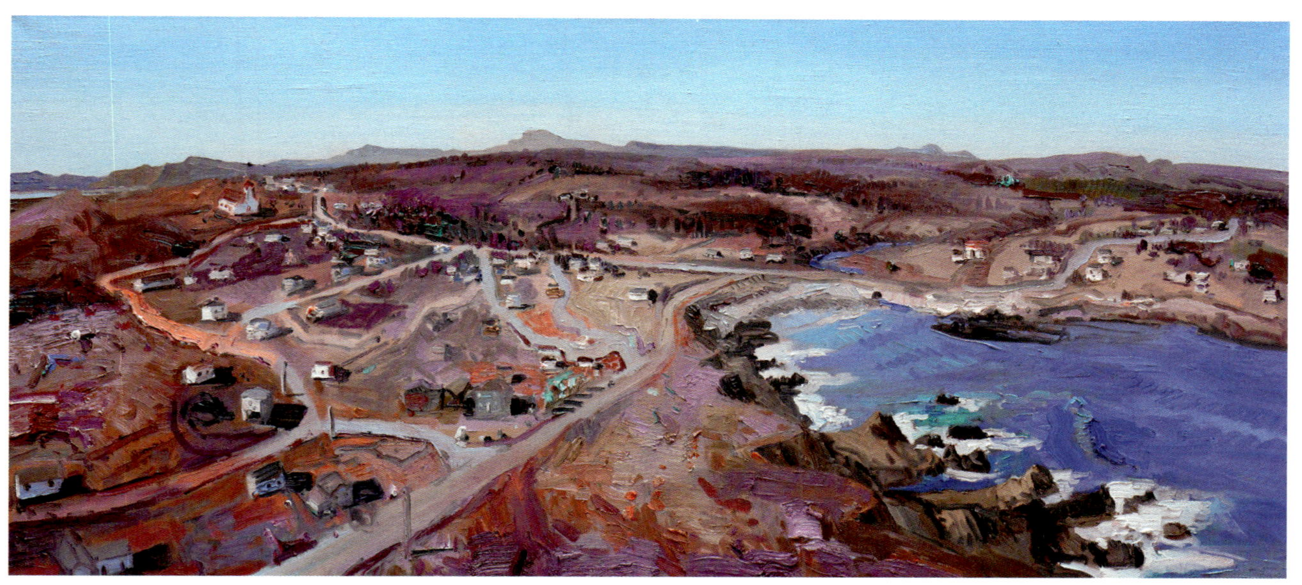

Broad Cove 2016
oil on linen
22″ × 48″

I am travelling through time. Late September, and I am naked and hugely pregnant at the roaring Archibald Falls. I want a photograph, so I climb the slimy lime green boulders, the sun shoots spears through the trees. My toes cramp from hanging on.

Can you just take the picture? I say to the father of my baby. Take the picture. Did you get it? Take the picture!

She drew a foot back and kicked me so hard, *kapow*, down low. How red everything was.

The biggest bubble bursts! The second won't get past the deck.

I gush forwards: my daughter is five? Eight? We are at Broad Cove, the sand almost black, the capelin rolling, dull like pewter, in the tumbling wave.

A man with a salt beef bucket, full to the lip with blood and solidified fat, tosses brine out toward the waves, *pickle* he calls it.

Slap-slap, the clotted fat and pork blood hits the water. The stink of capelin baking in the heat, panting so fast.

They go mad for the pickle, the man says. Capelin writhing, flip-flopping. And I am crazed too. I want that salty blood in my mouth, my eyes, I want it flushing through my gills. I fling myself into the air, confused by the single-mindedness of wanting, and there is my daughter on the shore, in soaked canvas sneakers. Later she breathes on the car window, draws a heart with her fingertip, *squeak, squeak,* and drops into sleep. Sand caked to her shins.

Everybody sings "Happy Birthday" and my father-in-law says, Isn't this nice. When my husband takes a picture, my father-in-law says, Will you put that thing away?

And then I am the hiss and flame of the propane lamp. There's no electricity, and the water comes from a well. There's a ring of stones where we buried the dog wrapped in my husband's favourite sweater, a note in the pocket. The last bubble floats above the lilac tree. My husband turns the dial on the propane lamp—the flame goes out and I am extinguished. ■

WILL FERGUSON
ABOVE CALGARY

2019 | **oil on linen, 48″ × 54″**

THE OPENING OF Will Ferguson's novel *419* starts with a car plunging into snowy darkness from a road in Calgary, near the upper right of this painting, in the heights overlooking the city. The book won the 2012 Scotiabank Giller Prize and was a departure from Will's earlier comedic novels, memoirs, and travel writing. He has won the Stephen Leacock Medal for Humour three times, for *Generica* (later retitled *Happiness*) in 2002, *Beauty Tips from Moose Jaw* in 2005, and *Beyond Belfast* in 2010.

Will's grandfather immigrated to Canada from Scotland with his three brothers, all of whom subsequently died in a coal mine collapse. He quit mining and started to work for the Canadian National Railway. Will's father was born in Saskatchewan, and his mother was from Burnaby. They settled in Fort Vermilion, on the Peace River, about 800 miles northwest of Edmonton. Will was born there, just below the sixtieth parallel. He says this is where the northern lights are the strongest. He and his friends would sometimes snowshoe across the frozen river with the idea of staying overnight in a shelter, but most often they'd come home the same evening. They were never the outdoorsmen they thought they were.

Will left Fort Vermilion when he was sixteen, still in high school, and began a long period of travelling the world. He graduated from film school in Toronto and finally settled in Calgary, in the neighbourhood that is in the bottom part of his portrait, nestled between the Elbow River and the downtown office towers. **/JH**

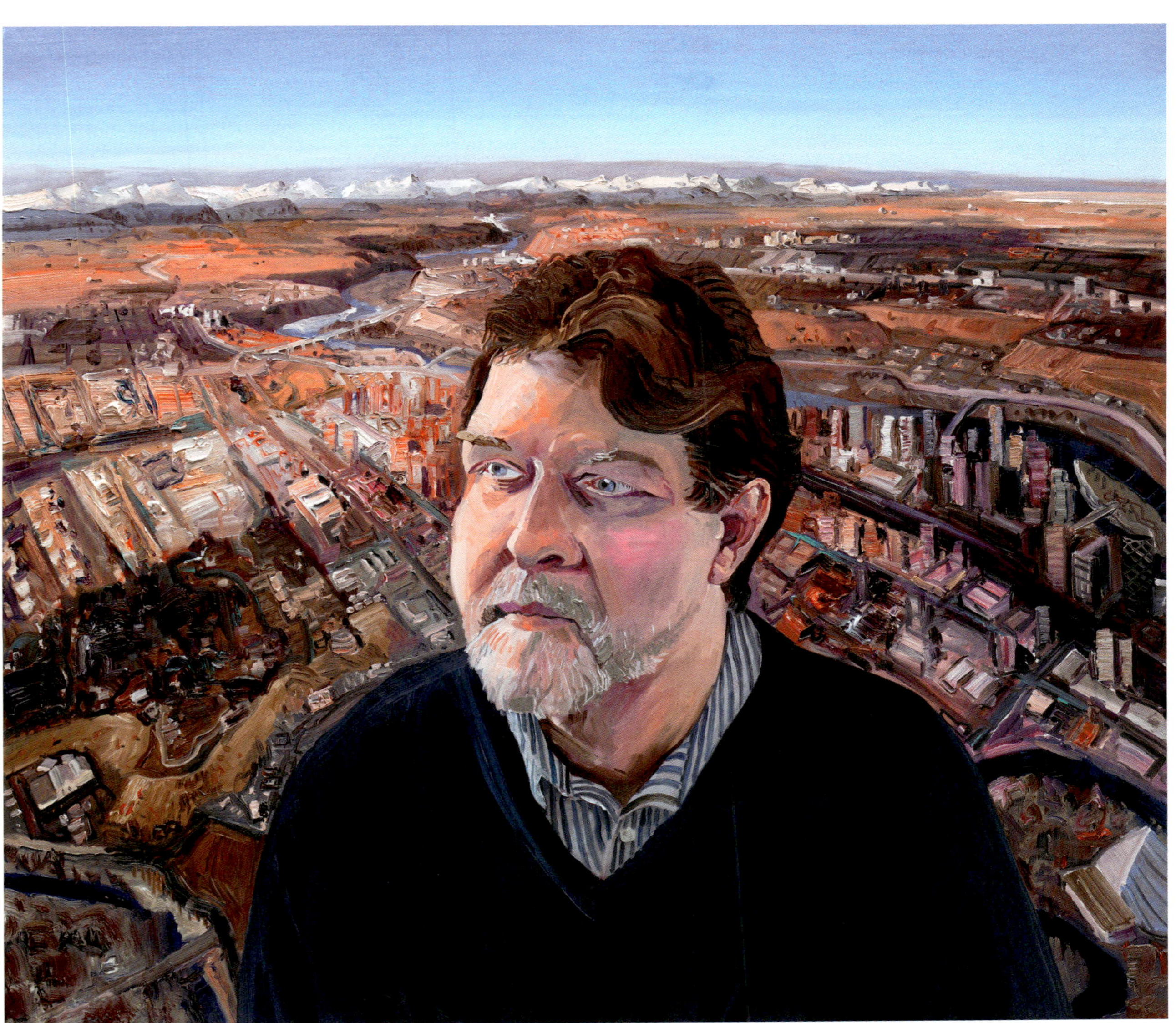

WILL FERGUSON

Village People

I GREW UP IN Northern Alberta, in a former fur-trading post closer to the Arctic Circle than the American border, and I've always felt that I immigrated *to* Canada. Lost in the middle of the boreal forest, Canada was a southern nation. And so, when my wife and I settled in Calgary to raise a family under the big skies of the Prairies, after a few years in the Maritimes, it was all vaguely exotic. But if I was expecting swaggering cowpokes, pie-sized belt buckles, and straw-chewing girls in Daisy Dukes, I was sorely disappointed. Calgary was and is a crisp city of glass towers and sandstone storefronts. A city of common sense (usually) and meritocracy (ditto), it remains a very liveable space, even if we only ever get to the mountains when we have guests in town.

We moved to the city's Mission neighbourhood in 1999, walking distance to downtown but still with the feel and appeal of a self-contained village. In fact, for many years, it was a village: Rouleauville, home of Calgary's original French Catholic mission. The clean lines of St. Mary's, more formally the Cathedral of the Immaculate Conception of the Blessed Virgin Mary, still mark the historic heart of the community, even if the livelier section is now along 4 Street.

We lived above 4 Street, formerly Broadway, near a turn in the Elbow River. From there, we watched the Lilac Festival morph from

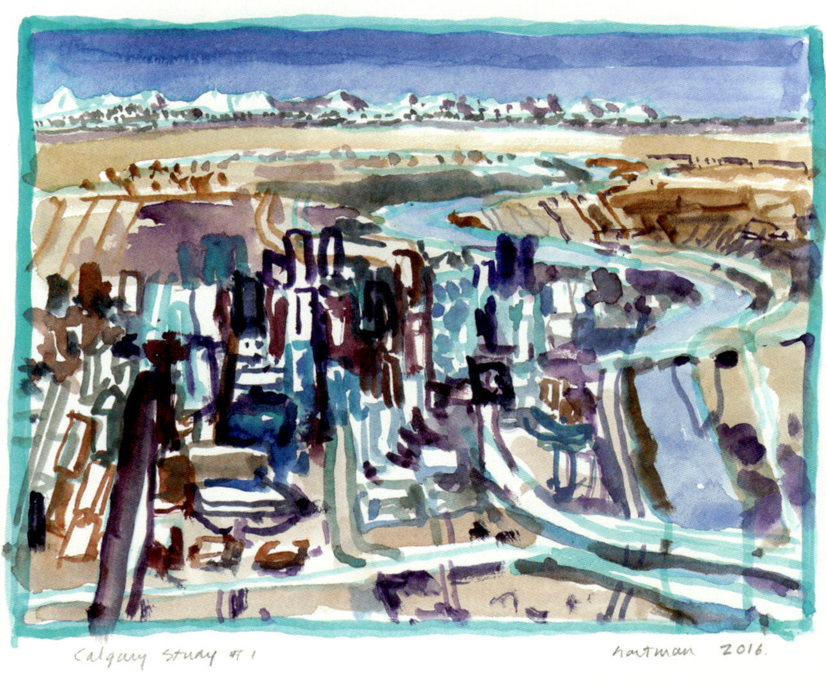

Calgary Study #1 2016
watercolour on paper
9″ × 11.25″

a quaint neighbourhood event to the sprawling pedestrian circus it is today. We saw the shape of the area slowly change, as smaller shops were knocked down and replaced by clunkier, bigger buildings. Yet the spirt of Mission endured. Calgary has always been an Etch A Sketch city, constantly erasing and rewriting itself.

Our kids went to the old Cliff Bungalow School, now an arts centre, and on Sundays we'd wander through Lindsay Park and Roxboro. We've since moved to Garrison Woods, a converted military barracks recast as a village-within-the-city, but the four years we spent in Mission remain formative, both for my wife and me and for our kids. Even if there were very few straw-chewing girls in Daisy Dukes. ■

GEORGE ELLIOTT CLARKE ABOVE THREE MILE PLAINS

2018 | **oil on linen, 60″ × 66″**

WHEN I ASKED George Elliott Clarke if I could paint his portrait, he replied, "I can only say yes. Paint me." We were off to a great start.

George grew up in Halifax and spent many weekends and holidays in Three Mile Plains, near Windsor, Nova Scotia. His mother's family has lived in this area for a very long time. He refers to himself as "Africadian," a term he coined to describe the Black population of Nova Scotia. They first arrived in 1783.

George is a poet, and among his many honours and awards, he won the Governor General's Award in 2001 for *Execution Poems*. This book and its companion novel, *George and Rue*, tell a story of his family in Three Mile Plains, and their relationship with the larger town of Windsor and with the more distant city of Halifax.

When I went to the area, I wasn't sure which house on Green Street belonged to George's grandmother. I eventually stopped and started to sketch what I thought was the right one. A minivan pulled up beside me, the window rolled down, and a woman who looked remarkably like George asked what I was doing. I told her. She smiled and said I had the right house, and then drove on. **/JH**

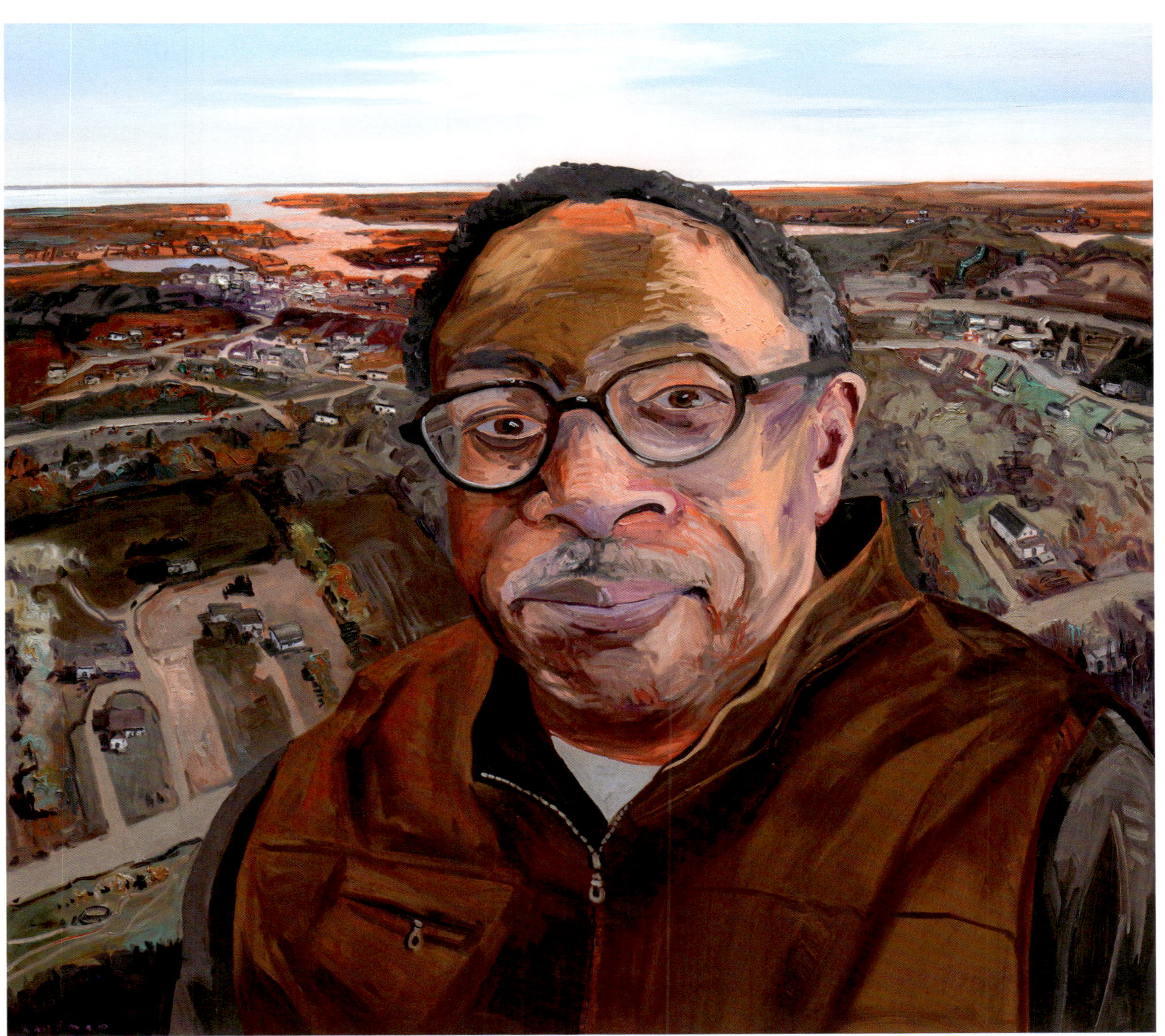

GEORGE ELLIOTT CLARKE

Green Street, Newport Station, Three Mile Plains

PETER E. MCKERROW'S *A Brief History of the Coloured Baptists of Nova Scotia* (1895) points out that many Black Refugees of the War of 1812–15, though scattered about mainland Nova Scotia, congregated in particular locales termed Three Mile Plains (including Panuke Road) and Five Mile Plains (including Green Street), collectively dubbed Windsor Plains, situated in West Hants. This historic, rural Africadian (African–Nova Scotian) enclave is located southeast of Windsor, but sixty-five kilometres northwest of Halifax.

McKerrow's history says there were enough Africadians around to support the establishment of an African Baptist church, now known as Windsor Plains United Baptist Church, as early as 1824. This foundation date is important, for it precedes Saint Richard Preston's establishment of Cornwallis Street Baptist Church in Halifax by eight years, suggesting that the founders of the Windsor Plains church just couldn't wait for London-baptized Father Preston to gather local Believers together himself.

Nevertheless, Satan be formidable in Nova Scotia, so church memberships be damned: the black folks got used as cheap labour, accused of congenital criminality, and abused as illiterates.

Such ill-usage goes back a long way. The notoriously racist, but internationally famous Bluenose writer Thomas Chandler

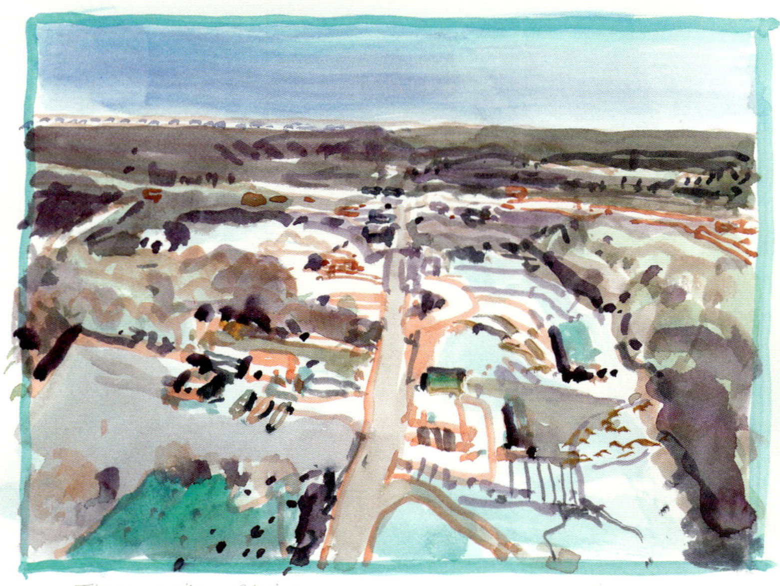

Three Mile Plains 2018
watercolour on paper
9.25″ × 11.25″

Haliburton (1796–1865) likely grew up with one or two slaves about, thus helping to justify his own lifelong belief that "Negro slavery" was a mighty fine way to run an economy.

In 1815, on his tour of "Acadie," Monsignor Joseph-Octave Plessis observed, in French, that the Windsor Plains blacks were "extremely numerous"—poor in dress, poor in cuisine, and poor in wages, but always workin' very, very, very, extra hard.

The folks who came to the Plains bore surnames like Croxen, Fletcher, Gray, Hamilton, Johnson, Paris, Upshaw, and States. That last surname is noteworthy because it may be a name that ex-slaves chose for themselves, to remember from whence they had come, and

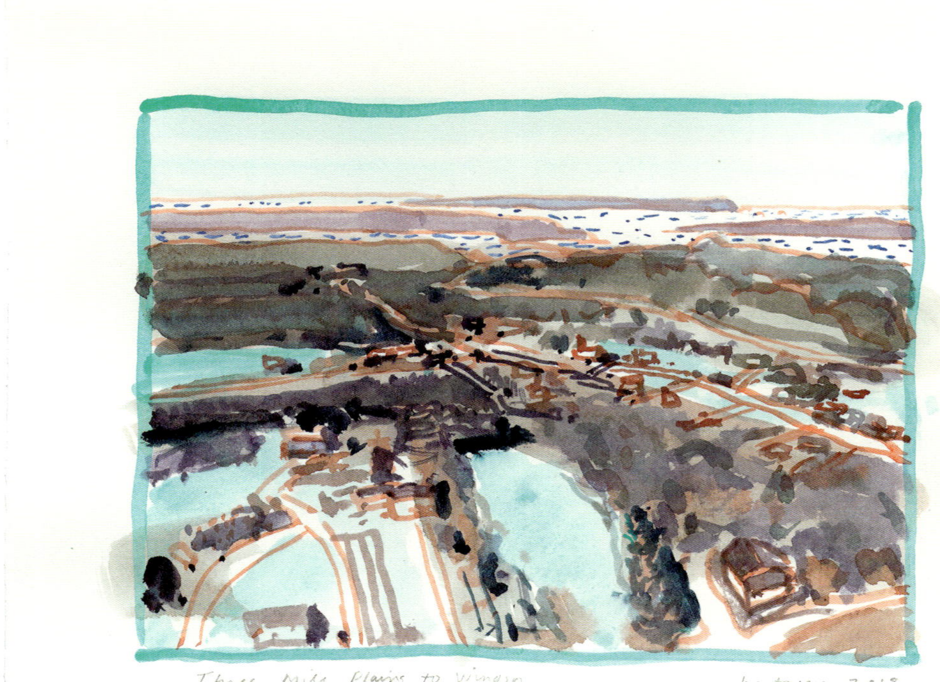

Three Mile Plains to Windsor 2018
watercolour on paper
9.25″ × 11.25″

not to remember ex-masters (and to confuse anyone who was hunting them down to try and return them to slavery).

Now, "Windsor Plains" is actually a misnomer. Rather, it is a series of hills and plateaus, both of which can sustain very small-scale crops, livestock rearing, and woodcutting. On the eastern side of the Plains, there are gypsum quarries.

I didn't grow up on Green Street, which is in Newport Station (a train mail stop some fifty years ago). I was born in Windsor, but grew up in Halifax. However, I still feel connected to Windsor Plains because I own three-quarters of an acre in Three Mile Plains, just diagonal to my late mother's girlhood home—still standing.

It's where John Milton and Nat Turner, Bob Dylan and Bessie Smith all infused my imagination with Biblical, bluesy ballads, as a teen poet, composing verses trying to unite apocalyptic sermonizin', trains braying or baying through the night, plus gals smellin' of molasses and kisses full of rum.

Also, I'm part Cherokee, part Mi'kmaq—an Afro-Métis like most of the black-brown folks who hail from Windsor Plains. Racists be damned! ■

KATHERINE GOVIER ABOVE MT. RUNDLE

2017 | **oil on linen, 60″ × 66″**

AS I WAS PAINTING Katherine Govier's portrait, I was reading *The Three Sisters Bar and Hotel*, her wonderful 2016 novel set in Banff and Canmore, or more precisely in a version of Canmore that includes elements of Banff. Some characters seem to me entirely fictional, and others are clearly related to historic figures that are part of the oral and written history of Alberta's mountain culture.

It is twenty kilometres from Banff to Canmore, and one mountain, Mount Rundle, occupies the entire distance. I have placed Katherine above the eastern edge of Banff, where the Bow River winds along the mountain's base. Canmore is the distant town in the upper left. I imagine that Katherine has listened to the stories that bubble up from these communities, so I painted a hand cupped behind her ear. She told me that Jimmy Simpson, the famous guide, and Mary Vaux Walcott, the astounding late nineteenth-century photographer who documented the glaciers of the Rockies, both turned into characters in the novel. I painted Jimmy in the lower right corner and Mary in the lower left. Mary Schäffer Warren, the early explorer, is painted sideways above Mary Vaux Walcott, even though Katherine says that she does not appear in the novel.

We all tell stories, each a little different. **/JH**

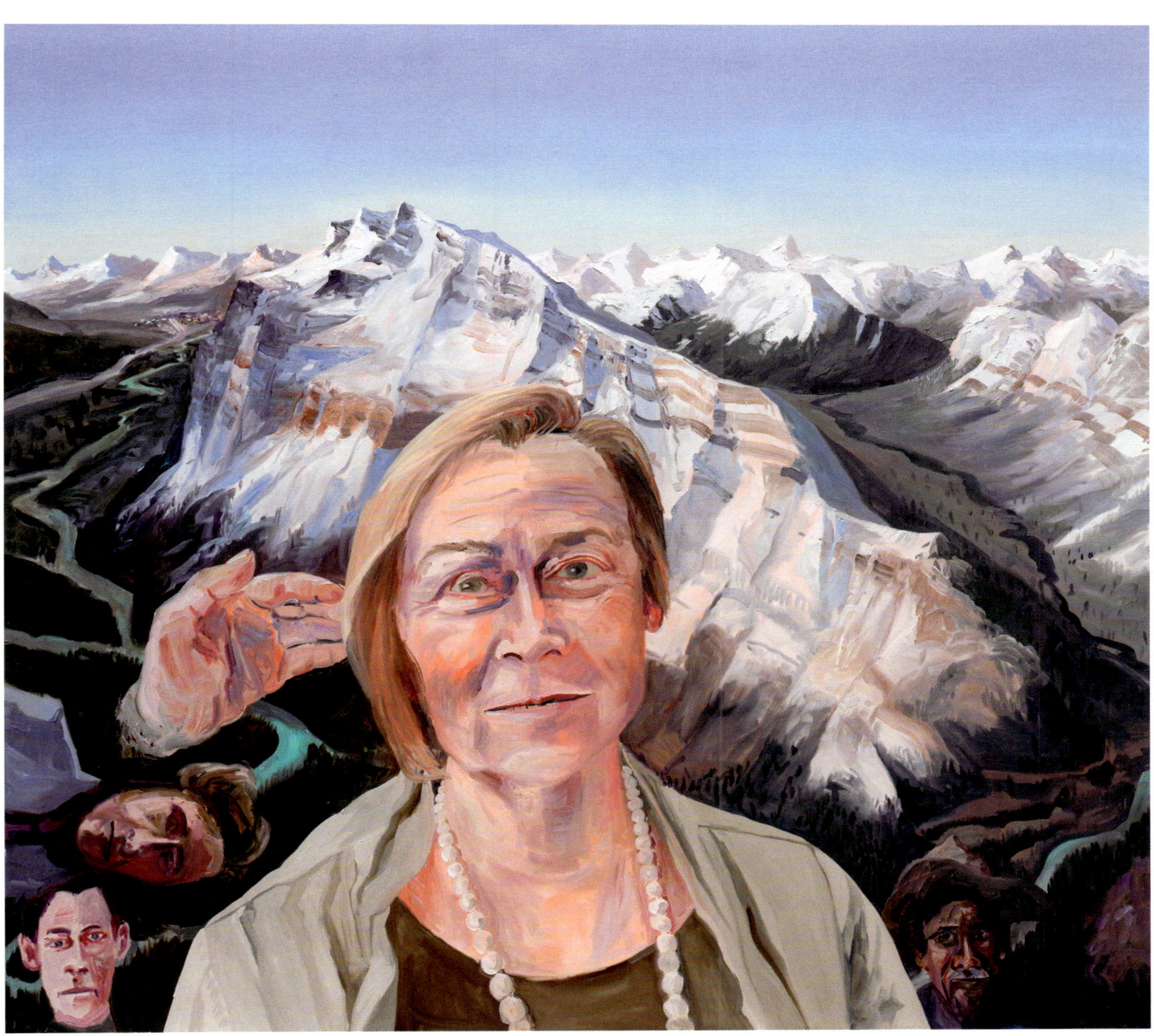

KATHERINE GOVIER

Splendid Isolation

THE WINDING TURQUOISE LINE that starts in the mountains, passes through Banff, and carries on down to Canmore, is my favourite river, the Bow. In high school, my friends and I sped alongside it in Dad's Karmann Ghia, bought to honour his mid-life crisis. Since my own, I have kayaked, walked, biked, camped, and waded that line, and fished on its banks. It is a powerful narrative, the river. Born at Bow Glacier, it pours down into Bow Lake, where Jimmy Simpson, with his beat-up Mountie hat, built his legacy, Num-Ti-Jah Lodge. The Bow slides through the upheavals and white tops and forests, often twinned with the highway—which may well be the nemesis of these wild places.

To make its way out of the grandeur, the river has to get around Rundle, a triangular upsurge of striated rock that separates Banff and its tourist glitter from Canmore and its mining past. By falls and meandering decline, it leaves the wild parts, only to become trapped by dams and bridges, turned subject and sad and giving up its trout. It joins with a half-dozen other rivers and eventually dumps into Hudson Bay. I like that: ultimately, it keeps its northerliness.

But the time in the Rocky Mountains is the Bow River's glory days.

There is an excellent loneliness in the Rockies. I feel it. Could rest my head in that cupped hand. We are all, somehow, alone here against the scale of the nearest mountain. We are always on a level, halfway up, at a peak, or traversing a scree slope: It is how one meets the mountains and discovers one's smallness. It is restful to be so dominated.

Many come to prove themselves, some to transform. Others come to be in the presence of spirits. Mary Schäffer and Mary Vaux were what we would call indomitable women. They could not be dominated, at least not by men. But they were by the mountains. No question. Seduced, carried away, and in thrall. You can give yourself to mountains.

Silence is required though.

There is a story Jimmy Simpson told of himself, on his trapline, alone under a ridge on a wintry night. He heard music, a symphony of violins, sweeping toward him and over his head. There was no radio in those days—no way to explain the onrushing melody—but he knew what he heard.

I think of the splendid isolation of the early white settlers. And of a generation later—my parents alone in a canoe on Bow Lake. No one else. Of myself riding a rattling bus with side loads of skis up to Sunshine Village. I had to get out on the hairpin turns and help push. Now there are gondolas and parking lots full of cars. The past is further away, and so is the silence. ■

DOUGLAS COUPLAND AT PARK ROYAL MALL

2018 | **oil on linen, 48″ × 54″**

DOUGLAS COUPLAND GREW UP in West Vancouver, where he now lives. He studied to be a sculptor, not a writer, at the Emily Carr Institute of Art and Design, in Vancouver. In 1991, after spending two years living and writing in the Mojave Desert, his first novel, *Generation X*, was published, a book that would make him famous. He has continued to publish regularly to critical acclaim and international attention.

In 2000, Douglas returned to his training as a visual artist and resumed his career with major Canadian and international exhibitions and public commissions. My favourite, perhaps because I drive by it so frequently, is *Monument to the War of 1812*, near Fort York in Toronto.

I visited him in West Vancouver on a dark, wet November evening. He lives in a home designed by Ron Thom, the great modernist architect. It is in its original configuration—many rooms each at slightly different levels, and none overly large. The library and the living room are filled with his collection of pop culture artifacts, collected in depth and carefully installed by category. Doug has allowed the trees on the property to grow to the point that the house is hidden, as is the view from inside. Over coffee, beside the open fire in the living room, he tells me that if the world is divided into cliff dwellers and cave dwellers, then he is the latter. **/JH**

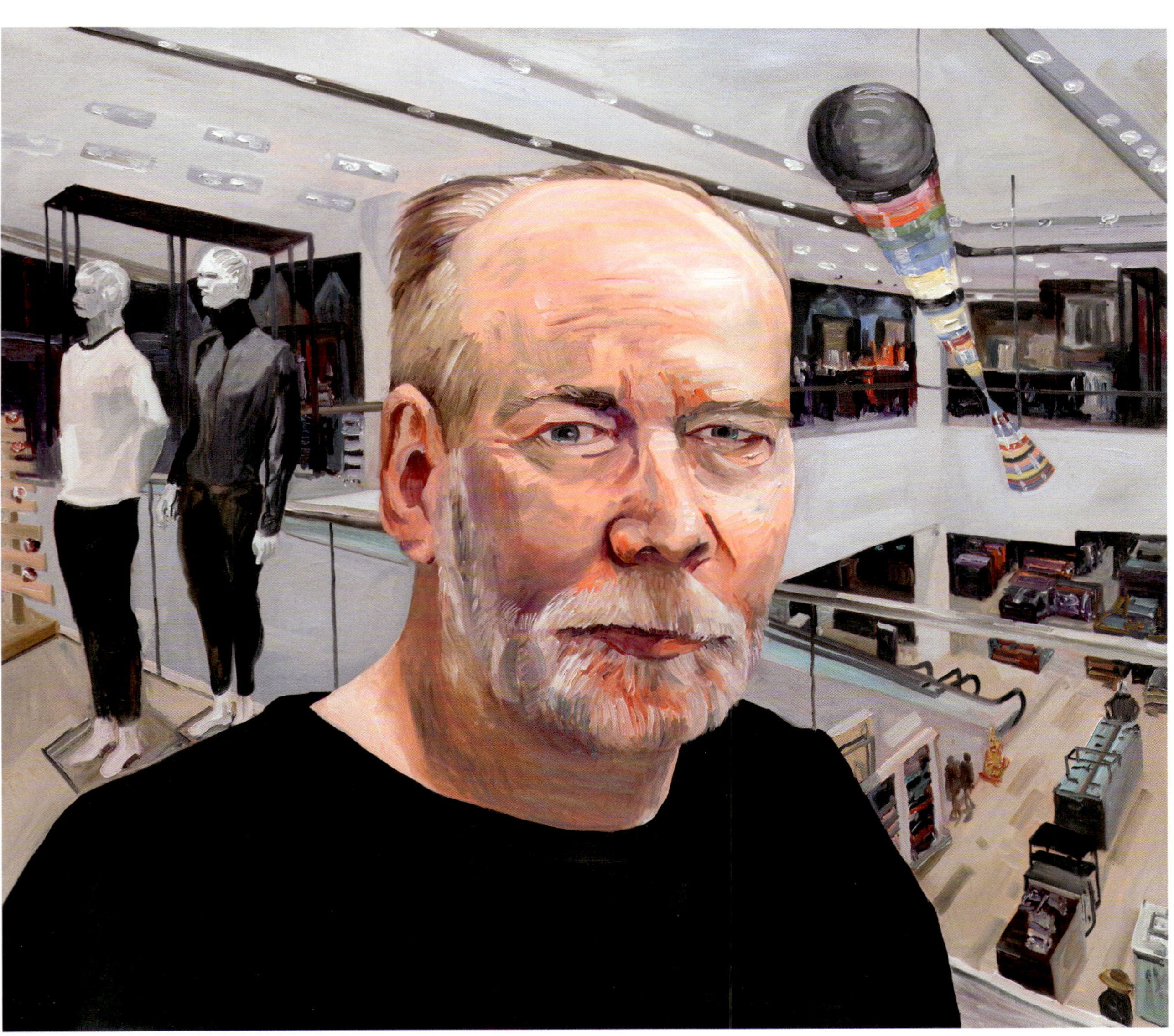

DOUGLAS COUPLAND

Park Royal

CANADA'S FIRST INDOOR shopping mall was Park Royal in West Vancouver, where I grew up. It was part of four thousand acres sold for three beans to the Guinness family in the early twentieth century. My family lived up the mountain in a Guinness development called the British Properties. Its main streets were actually logging roads from around 1900, and in the 1970s the Properties were labelled by people downtown as Martini Hill—which would have been great, but it was actually just an alpine *Brady Bunch* prison until you got your driver's licence two weeks after your sixteenth birthday. My first job was when I was fourteen, bussing tables at Ricky's Pancake House, at Park Royal, counting the days and tips until I could buy a car and be free.

When it opened in 1950, Park Royal was a paragon of West Coast modernity: clean lines, delicate concrete brise soleils, ample parking, natural lighting, all with piped-in music. Massive indoor planters were home to then-exotic scheffleras and dieffenbachia, planted in the middle of a white terrazzo strip that ran between Eaton's and SuperValu. In 1970, the north side of Park Royal was redesigned in the spirit of Rhoda Morgenstern's apartment, tiled with funky dark terracotta tiles all glazed with sienna and orange. All-natural lighting was removed.

Around 1985, Park Royal became the Winchester House of shopping malls, commencing its ongoing tradition of every ten years doing large, awkward, weirdly ten-years-out-of-date renovations. Above-ground roadways are regularly lopped off, becoming truncated ghost roads ending at concrete walls like the sectioning off of Cold War Berlin. Parts of the mall are seemingly ignored and can resemble Beirut minus bullet holes. To go from A to B within Park Royal requires the Knowledge of a London cabbie. And yet the mall seems to be thriving. Go mall!

In 2013, Simons, based in Quebec City, was building a new department store from scratch in Park Royal—"from scratch" not being a phrase often heard within Park Royal's perpetually remorphed forms. Simons was interested in having an artist residing in West Van do a work for the space, and it was a nice fit for me. The piece is called *Bow Tie* and hangs in the store's central atrium. I like it because when you look at it, your brain thinks, "What the hell is that? It looks like it wants to shatter and explode. Is it real? How did it come into existence?" The centre of gravity in any cone is one-third up from its base, which is where suspending wires attach to the piece. Where the two cones look like they're attacking each other, there's no pressure between them at all. They're kissing, and if you look at it upside down, *Bow Tie* works just as well as right-side up. It would work in outer space. It's a piece from the future, always my favourite place. ■

KEVIN MAJOR ABOVE THE EASTPORT PENINSULA

2018 | **oil on linen, 48″ × 54″**

ON VICTORIA DAY Weekend in 1997, I travelled with Kevin Major and his sons, Luke and Duncan, from their home in St. John's to Sandy Cove, on Newfoundland's Eastport Peninsula. Kevin wanted to show me the community where he had spent his formative years as a writer. We stayed in a friend's cottage, close to the edge of the sand cliffs on the left side of this painting. We ate lobster, looked for capelin, and climbed the nearby Louil Hills, which gave us a view out over the entire peninsula. It was here where Kevin created *Stagehead*, a journal that collected and published the stories of the area's people. This was part of a cultural awakening across Newfoundland in the 1970s that celebrated outport life and traditions.

I now realize that collecting and publishing these stories was an important part of Kevin's beginnings as a writer. In 1978, when he was twenty-nine, his first novel, *Hold Fast*, won the Governor General's Award and was selected for the Hans Christian Andersen Honour List. An auspicious start to a distinguished career. **/JH**

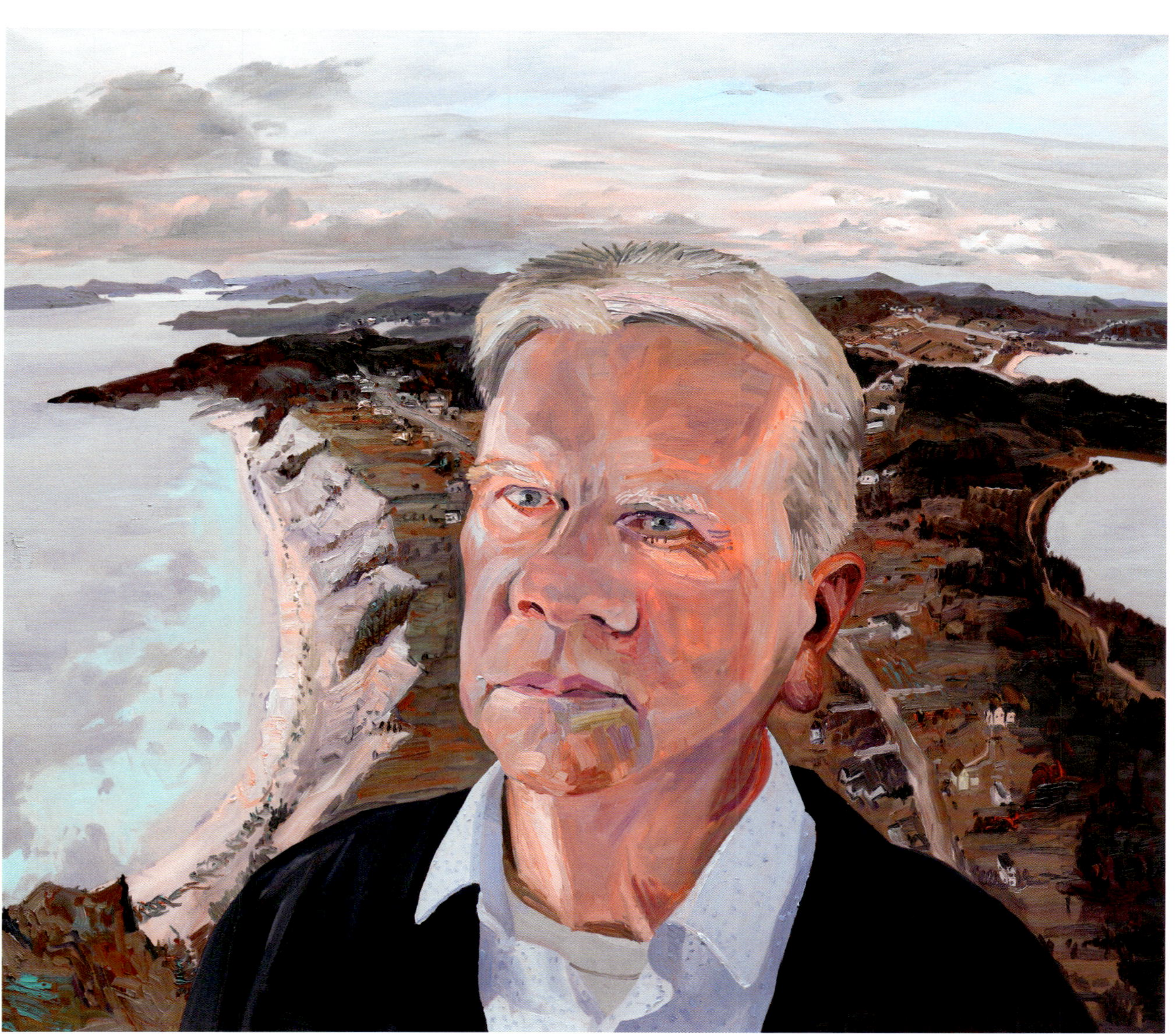

KEVIN MAJOR

The Choice

WE CANNOT CHOOSE where we're born. Through willpower and circumstance, we can choose where we live.

I purposely sought out the Eastport Peninsula. It was the first week of September 1974, and I was going there to teach. There were other places in Newfoundland I could have gone, but I had decided the Eastport Peninsula was where I wanted to be. I had ambitions as a writer and a strong sense that this place was going to suit me very well.

Driving down the access road from the Trans-Canada, I crested a hill that revealed a remarkable vista, deep inlets of Bonavista Bay defining both sides. I saw the sun beginning to set in the rear-view mirror, and in front of me the moon had chosen the same hour to rise. Landscape had never promised me more. The road twisted down to a causeway that led to the seven communities scattered across the peninsula. A curious mix of names—Sandringham, Eastport, Happy Adventure, Sandy Cove, St. Chad's, Burnside, Salvage—and not one with more than a few hundred people. I will never be so attached to a place as I became to it, driving about in my black Celica, heading for hills to climb, seeking panoramas of the outports below.

I made the Eastport Peninsula home for the next sixteen years. I came to know it through my students and their parents and grand-parents. I married, and Anne and I had two children to run about its brilliant beaches, scooping up capelin and poking at bonfires. Home was rural Newfoundland, not without its intrigues, and, true enough, a fine place to start a career as a writer. I published five books, and my time there would impact many more.

Now nearly thirty years after we left, I don't often go back. When I do it's as if we had never moved. Strange, to be so attached to a place and then give it up and make another life for yourself somewhere else, somewhere very different. The Eastport Peninsula generously gave me what I wanted—at the point in my life I needed it most.

I sometimes hear voices from that past. I hear Angus bantering on about setting rabbit snares, "tailin' slips" as he called it. "Got to get yer gut to the ground." Mac, his father, adding, "If you got a good slip, he'll never bus' out if he's on a growed standard, no way in the world." "Got to know what yer at," says Angus. Don't want to be "makin' the devil's own job of it." Such richness of language for a writer.

I miss it. When I think about it, I do. But I don't often think about it, because another life eclipsed the one I had outgrown. A life more suited to me in many ways. Still, when the time comes, when I'm "drove up for time," as Mac might have put it, when, like the rabbit, "there's not a draft left in 'en," is it here that I'd want my ashes scattered? ■

SUSAN SWAN AND THE WESTERN ISLANDS

2017 | **oil on linen, 66″ × 60″**

SUSAN SWAN AND I grew up in the same town of Midland, Ontario. We shared much the same childhood experience, and we definitely share the same home landscape—the low rocky islands of the eastern shore of Georgian Bay, the beaches of Nottawasaga Bay, and, of course, Midland itself. This is the setting of my two favourite books by Susan, *The Last of the Golden Girls* and *The Western Light*. (She may not have set her latest novel, *The Dead Celebrities Club*, on Georgian Bay, but I look forward to reading it nonetheless.)

I wanted to get all the local places that are part of her writing into one painting, and after two boat trips to the Western Islands, I had the sketches I needed. But it was a comment that Susan made about the old local library that made me realize I needed to include the red brick building. This led me to create a rather fantastical backdrop for her portrait, with distortions of scale and a very high viewing point—still true to our shared home landscape. **/JH**

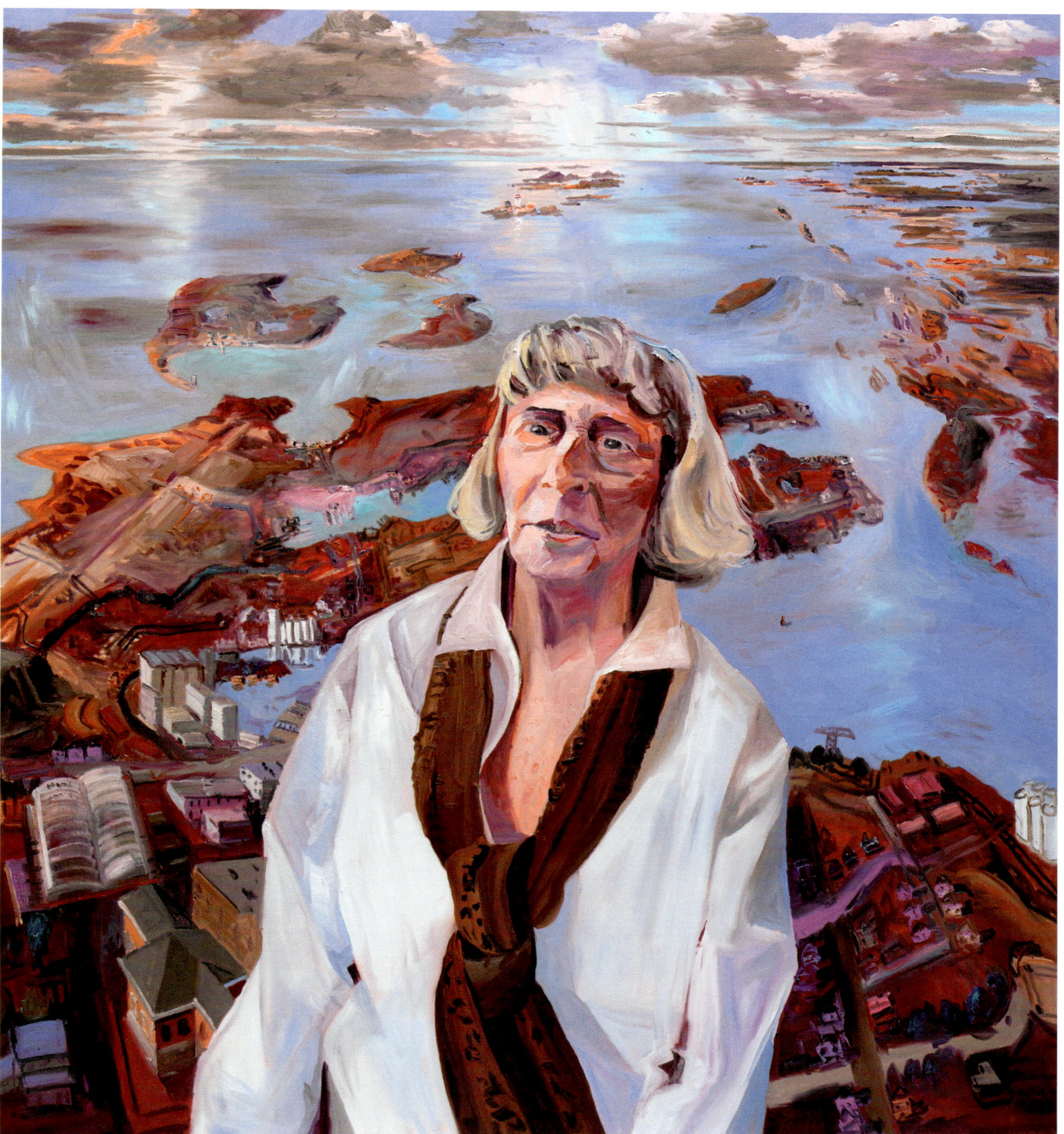

SUSAN SWAN

Portals of Mystery and Knowledge

THE LATE RICHARD B. WRIGHT and I used to talk about how the old Carnegie library in Midland shaped us as writers. So it's fitting that the building is in John Hartman's portrait, near my right elbow, right below the floating book. The red-brick library was an alternative space in a small Ontario town, where English Canadians were crazy for the Maple Leafs and French Canadians rooted for Les Canadiens. Midland's English-speaking mayor became so excited during NHL playoffs that his wife made him sit outside while she, listening on the radio, would signal the score to him through a window.

For me, the library sustained a passion that had nothing to do with hockey—the private thrill of reading. Located at the corners of First Street and Hugel Avenue, not far from the home of Miss Mullen, my grade one teacher, it was a capacious two-storey building with large arched windows overlooking both streets. As a child in the 1950s, I went three or four times a week, loading up with books from the children's section on the first floor. In grade seven, I was allowed to climb the stairs to the adult section, where I read everything—novels and books about history, science, and sex. I even read a self-improvement primer on how to win friends and influence people, by Dale Carnegie, no relation to the American steel magnate and philanthropist who funded the place. I took out so many books that Mr. Lee, the head librarian, made an exception to the rule for me: instead of just three books a week, I was allowed to take home six.

In 1967, the library moved into a larger space offered by Midland's old post office and customs house. That same year, I graduated from university and became a writer. My second novel, *The Last of the Golden Girls,* describes competitions for boys between girls and young women during summers on Georgian Bay, the pale blue body of water, sometimes called the sixth Great Lake, that serves as the portrait's backdrop. Lovely backlit clouds drift across the sky, while above my head, pink granite islands float eternally in the bay, offering a sense of freedom and mystical connection to anyone who goes there.

For me, the library and Georgian Bay were both portals. The library, with its shelves of unread books, took me on journeys where I learned what others had thought or done. The bay, meanwhile, gave me the chance to know myself from the inside. It bounced feelings back at you, and if you stayed long enough you could find out what you were made of. A spiritual education, in other words, lies in those bountiful rocky waters famous for jump-up weather and horizons that don't quit. (Like me, Hartman grew up on its shores, and he knows how to convey its haunting beauty.)

Mouse Bradford, the narrator in my novel *The Western Light* says it best:

> And before I knew it, I was telling my aunt about the generations of Bradford families who ran a fishing station near the lighthouse and brought the whitefish and lake trout over to Owen Sound, most of them never learning to swim. I wanted to cheer her up and make her love the bay the way I loved it . . . For me it was a deep down feeling of lastingness that has nothing to do with the water and the rocks. The Bay was closer than the stars, I explained, and every bit as remote and mysterious. ■

NEIL BISSOONDATH BESIDE THE ST. LAWRENCE RIVER

2018 | **oil on linen, 40″ × 46″**

NEIL BISSOONDATH WAS born in Arima, Trinidad, and came to Canada as an eighteen-year-old to study at York University, in Toronto. His interest in literature was encouraged at an early age by his mother and later by her brother, the writer V.S. Naipaul. Neil had early success with the publication of *Digging Up the Mountains,* a short story collection, but it was the publication of *A Casual Brutality* in 1989 that brought him commercial success and critical acclaim.

I visited Neil in Quebec City in February. It was cold and snowy. He had explained that he would like Parc de la Plage-Jacques-Cartier as part of his portrait, because it was where, in the dead of winter on a park bench beside the ice-jammed St. Lawrence River, he began to write, in longhand, the first draft of his novel *The Unyielding Clamour of the Night*. I visited the narrow strip of land the day before I went to Neil's home. I was a little unsure if I had the correct location, so Neil was happy to take me there again. We located the bench where he sat, and I photographed him at the exact site of this unlikely source of inspiration. The bench is behind Neil on the left side of the painting, but buried under snow. On the right side, the riverside path continues east toward the two great bridges that cross the St Lawrence. It is snowing. **/JH**

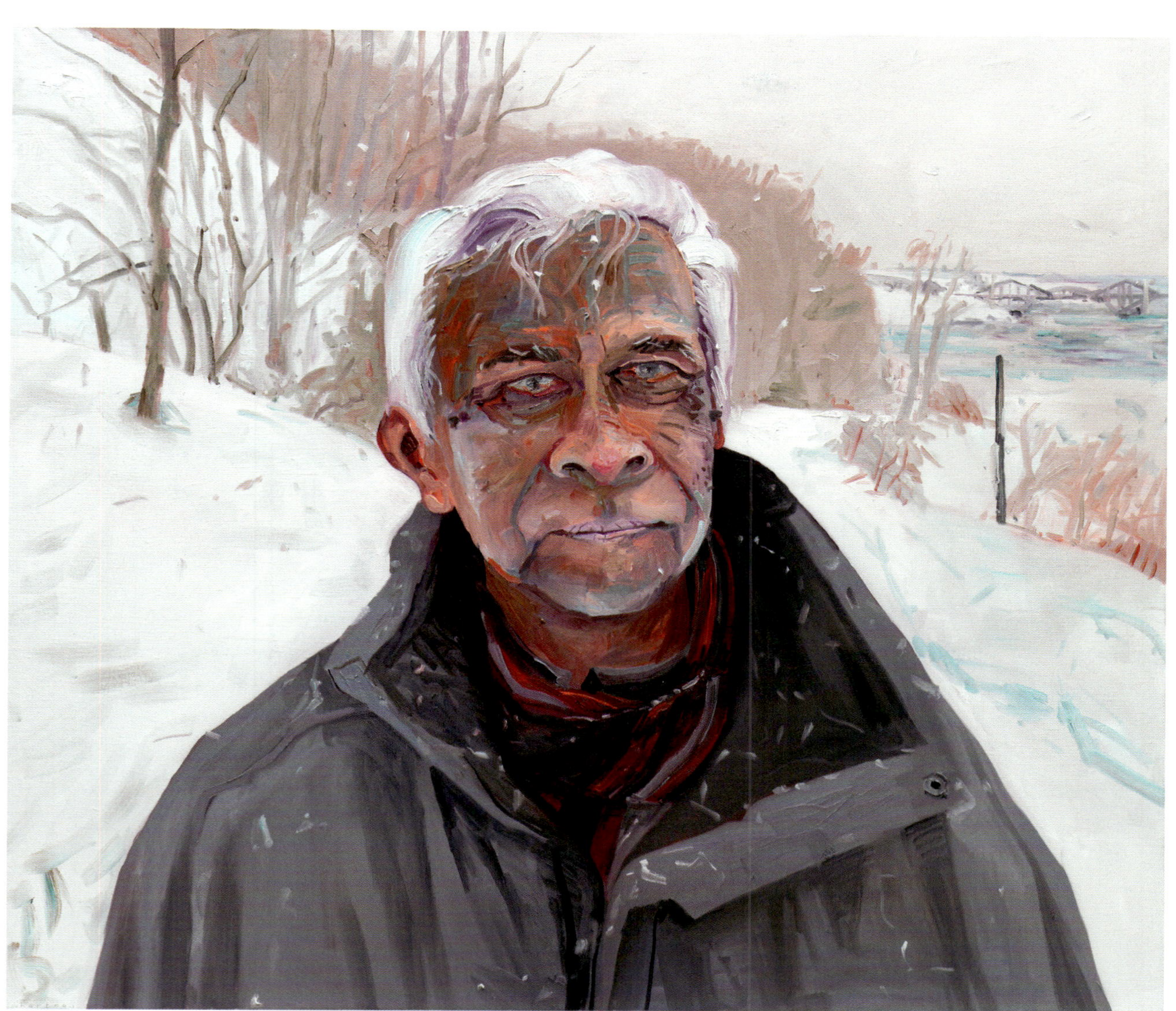

NEIL BISSOONDATH

The Park

THE ORIGIN OF Quebec City's name is subject to some uncertainty. Most sources agree it refers to the city's location on the St. Lawrence River—at the spot "where the river narrows." But does the word "Quebec" derive from Iroquois, Mi'kmaq, or Montagnais? And might it actually be Montagnais for "disembark," the Indigenous people calling to Jacques Cartier to leave his ship and set foot on dry land?

Geography would seem to settle it in favour of the narrowing of the river. A few kilometres downstream, the St. Lawrence (so dubbed because Cartier came across it on the saint's feast day in 1534) acquires the girth of an inland sea, its waist so wide the far shore appears to be on the other side of the world, beyond the horizon. It is to me an impressive and unsettling change, discomfiting in that it returns a part of me to the boy I was growing up in Trinidad, where I saw the horizon not as a portal to the larger world but as a barrier imprisoning me on the little island.

This is perhaps one reason I feel at peace at the Parc de la Plage-Jacques-Cartier (Cartier's name, like Samuel de Champlain's, is ubiquitous in the city), a two-and-a-half-kilometre beach created on the northern bank of the great river, not far from my home. The south shore is a manageable distance away. Past sailboats, cruise ships, and heavily laden freighters, houses and cars peek from its heavily forested slopes. It is suggestive of a massive land of promise and achievement beyond.

The park itself, bucolic in every season and unsullied by commerce, emerges at the base of a forested cliff. The lawns, paths, and beach that summon summer picnickers, walkers, and joggers give way to a cliché of colours in fall and then to a fantasy of snow and ice in winter, dry-docked sailboats replaced by a Coast Guard icebreaker clearing a channel for cargo ships. Thanks to the alchemy of light on water and the mischievousness of clouds, the beach is like a chameleon—one thing at one moment, another thing minutes later.

From here, the two bridges linking the shores—the century-old Pont de Québec and the Pont Pierre-Laporte, Canada's longest suspension bridge—perform a trompe l'oeil. Standing one beside the other, they appear to meld into one, their act of bonding both physical and allegorical.

All of this makes the Parc de la Plage-Jacques-Cartier a perfect place for a writer to access the internal drama of the imagination. While here, I frequently scribble a few lines essential to a character or a scene unrelated to my surroundings. Once, in the depths of a frigid February—amid three feet of snow and before a St. Lawrence rigid with ice—the opening pages of my novel *The Unyielding Clamour of the Night*, set in a hot and humid tropical country, wrote themselves.

I've lived here longer than in any other place. It is home.

Where the river narrows is a good place to land. ■

CARLEIGH BAKER ABOVE NEW BRIGHTON PARK

2018 | **oil on linen, 60″ × 66″**

CARLEIGH BAKER'S DEBUT short story collection, *Bad Endings*, won the 2017 City of Vancouver Book Award. It was also shortlisted for the Rogers Writers' Trust Fiction Prize. In a video made by the Writers' Trust, Carleigh says, "The unifying themes are bad decisions and transgressions, but also resilience. You've got to be pretty resilient if you are making a lot of bad decisions."

Carleigh asked me to paint Burrard Inlet, near New Brighton Park. She lives nearby and told me, "I like the mixture of nature and industry there."

This is one of the few places where residents can access the waterfront on this heavily industrialized stretch of the southern shore of Burrard Inlet. An urban park, popular with dog owners, it is hemmed in by the massive grain elevators to the left of Carleigh's head, by the rail lines on the right side, which feed the Port of Vancouver, and by container facilities below the bottom edge of the painting. Yet it is an exhilarating place to be, because it is beside the inlet's tidal waters. **/JH**

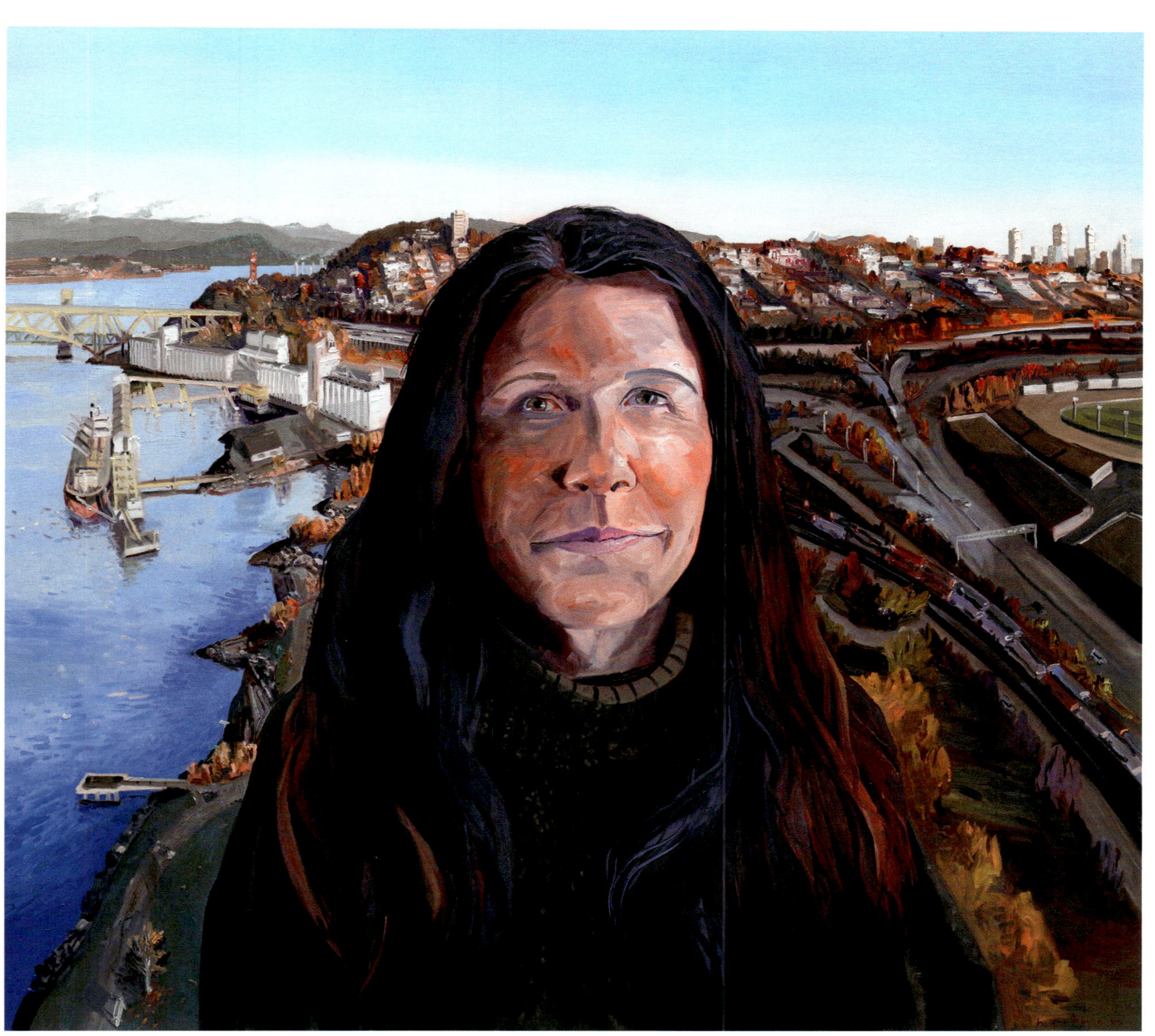

CARLEIGH BAKER

Here Vancouver Began

A PLAQUE AT New Brighton Park says, “Here Vancouver Began.” Which is not untrue. The first post office, hotel, telegraph, playing field, and museum were built by settlers at the Hastings Townsite. The plaque also says, “All was forest towering to the skies.” This, too, is mostly true. But like a Group of Seven painting, the image is all landscape and no people.

What the inscription does not acknowledge is that people were here long before “Vancouver began.” They remain today—the xʷməθkʷəy̓əm, Sḵwx̱wú7mesh, and səlilw̓ətaʔɬ peoples. The Sḵwx̱wú7mesh name for the surrounding area is X̱epx̱ápay̓ay, meaning “cedar trees.” This information did not make it onto the plaque.

Vancouver continues to be presented as having risen up from a majestic coastal forest devoid of humans, or at least humans of consequence. This convenient erasure makes its development seem like a noble and exciting enterprise, when the truth is far more complex. Settlers have long invoked the principle of *terra nullius*—nobody’s land—to claim that colonization was inevitable, even favourable, because no one (of consequence) lived here. And since Vancouver still has so much preserved nature, since we are still in many ways a “forest towering to the skies,” this erasure implies urban development was somehow a kinder, gentler form of colonialism.

Also not true. But it's a seductive idea for those who don't want to acknowledge that the city's history is one of displacement. It's a cozy dissonance.

Seeing my image painted over New Brighton Park creates another kind of dissonance. In a way, it presents the idea that I have some kind of claim to the land. I don't. I am a guest in this unceded place. I was born and raised on Stó:lō territory. My Métis family originally comes from Treaty 1 territory. My Icelandic family are settlers, uninvited guests. It's my responsibility to recognize that my presence here is a form of continued colonial violence.

I relate to New Brighton Park, a fifteen-minute walk from my apartment, because it's surrounded by heavy industry, on a border between what is currently called Vancouver and currently called Burnaby. As a Métis person, I also live between worlds. As an urban Indigenous person, I'm bonded to urban spaces, only a little "outdoorsy." As an artist and a low-income earner, I've been displaced to Hastings–Sunrise, one of the few affordable neighbourhoods left in Vancouver. But the displacement that is a result of gentrification is a relatively recent kind. This is unceded xʷməθkʷəy̓əm, Sk̲wx̲wú7mesh, and səlil̓wətaʔɬ land. I have no claim to it. I'm grateful to live here, but my gratitude is not enough.

The plaque at New Brighton Park also says that the Hastings Townsite was a resort destination—"the most fashionable watering place in British Columbia." As uninvited guests, we can't treat this land as a watering place. We're in a reciprocal relationship with it and its original inhabitants. We have responsibilities. ■

MICHAEL CRUMMEY ABOVE WESTERN BAY

2017 | **oil on linen, 48″ × 68″**

MICHAEL CRUMMEY WAS born in Buchans, a mining town in central Newfoundland at the headwaters of the Exploits River. The watershed of the Exploits is the setting for *River Thieves*, Michael's award-winning, best-selling debut novel. His fourth novel, *Sweetland*, explores mortality through the story of resettlement and an outport's denouement as a community. Michael is a wonderful storyteller, but he is also a prolific poet, publishing five collections since 1996.

It is my habit when visiting St. John's to visit the Ship Inn to listen to the live music. On my latest trip, the evening's program consisted of a "read-off" between poets and playwrights. Michael was reading for the poet's team, and each team had cheerleaders. Spouses, both male and female, dressed the part. It was a lot of fun. Afterward, I talked with Michael, I purchased the *Breakwater Book of Contemporary Newfoundland Poetry*, and I finished the evening at a bar on George Street, where I forgot my new book. When I returned next day to retrieve it, it was gone. St. John's loves its writers. **/JH**

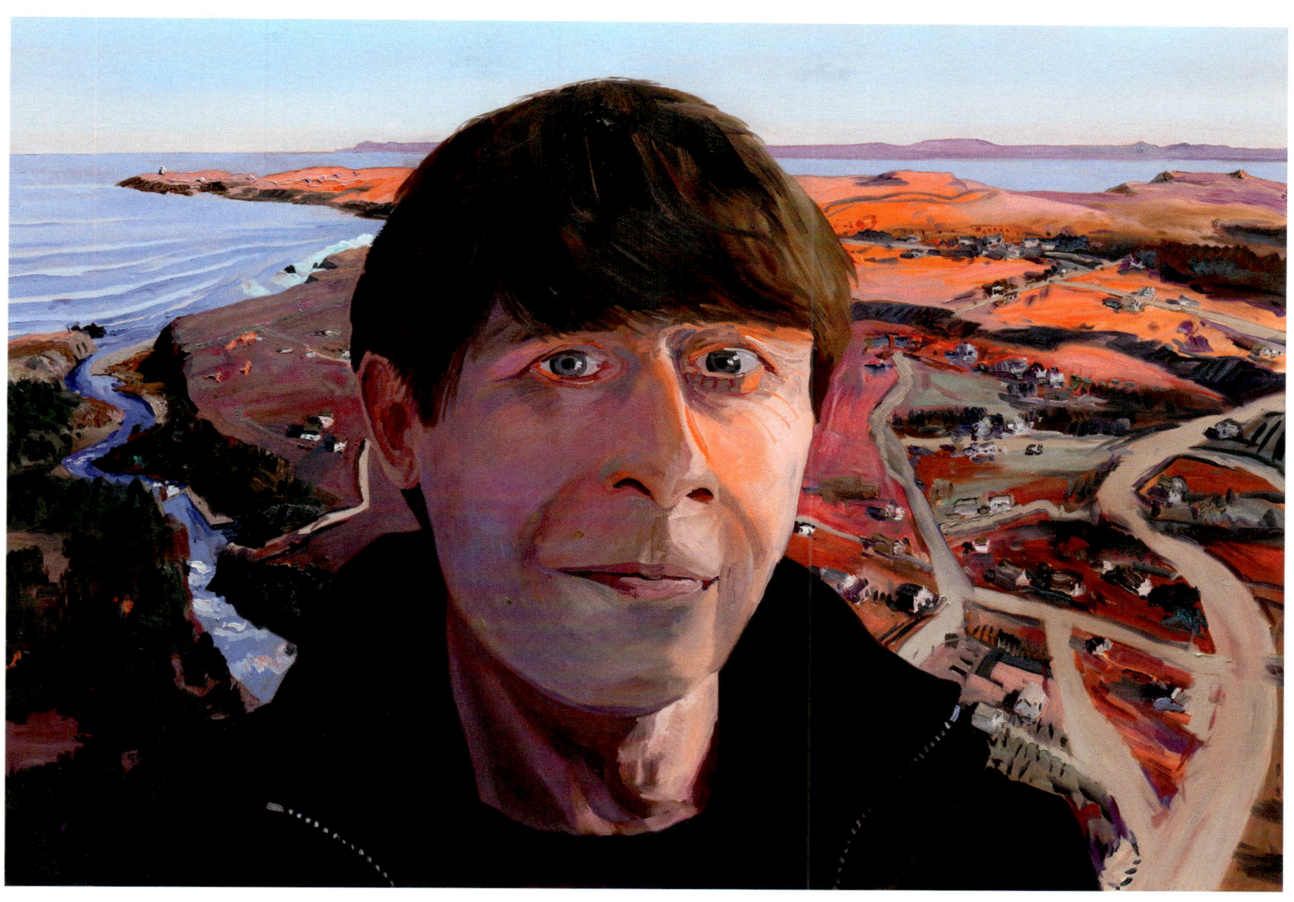

MICHAEL CRUMMEY

Next Door

THIS IS WESTERN BAY, on the north shore of Newfoundland's Conception Bay. When I was a youngster, my family used to come here to spend a week or so with my grandmother, in the house where my father was born and raised. People still kept livestock then; they cut hay and set gardens of potatoes and turnip and cabbage. I mooed at the cows and baaed at the sheep in the backyard fields. I spent time at the Overfalls, a swimming hole in the river over my right shoulder. Those annual visits ended when my Nan died. The house sat empty for decades, and it was torn down just after I moved back to Newfoundland from Ontario in 2001.

Somewhere behind my head is the house on the South Side Road that my wife, Holly, and I bought twelve years ago, next door to the Pink House, where Michael Winter spends his summers. The Dalton brothers were in their seventies when they sold the place to us, both men living in St. John's and getting too old to look after it. Holly and I showed up for our initial viewing with three youngsters in tow. The Daltons were strangers to me, but I discovered after the fact that Nan and my Aunt Helen used to walk up here to have tea with Mrs. Dalton when my aunt was a girl. I also discovered later that someone made a better offer on the house, but I think the Dalton brothers liked the idea of it going to someone they "knew." They liked the thought there would be kids in the house.

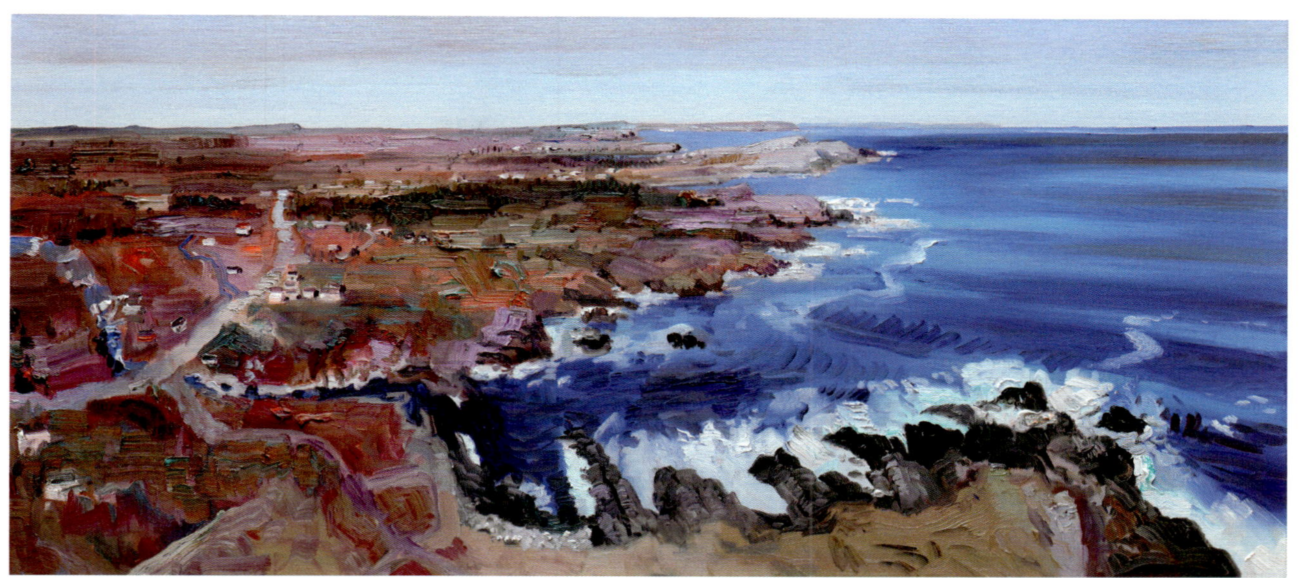

Blackhead to Western Bay, NF 2016
oil on linen
22″ × 48″

There was no official survey for the property, and creating one involved taking affidavits from the oldest people on the road, who could say when the place was built and what the generally accepted boundaries were. All of those folks have passed on in the years since.

There's cell coverage the entire length of the North Shore except for Western Bay, which sits in a black hole all its own for some reason. Our kids used to walk out to the highest point near the lighthouse—what they called Service Mountain—to text their friends back in St. John's. I've recently discovered that if I lay my phone on one corner of the desk in our upstairs bedroom when the weather is clear, I can get a couple of bars to send a note or call home. It's the same spot I set the laptop to poach on Michael Winter's Wi-Fi when he hooks it up each summer, the signal leaking across the empty lot between us. And that feels like just about the right level of "connectedness." Even as a kid, Western Bay seemed like a place apart to me, a little adjacent to my regular life. Next door to the modern world.

This may be a selfish thought, but I hope it never moves any closer. ■

MICHAEL WINTER
ABOVE BRADLEY'S COVE

2017 | **oil on linen, 60″ × 66″**

MICHAEL WINTER WAS very quick and clear with me: he wanted me to paint the community of Bradley's Cove as part of his portrait. Michael's home in Newfoundland is in the community of Western Bay, and if you walk out his door and down the road a short distance, you come to the path that will lead you, in about ten minutes time, to Bradley's Cove, or rather to the foundations of a few old buildings and at least one intact root cellar that were once part of a now-abandoned community.

When I walked to Bradley's Cove, I saw a barren and rough shoreline of black rock cliffs, pounded by the waves sweeping across Conception Bay. I sketched the view back toward Western Bay.

I returned to Western Bay and stood in front of Michael's house. I wondered, How much writing does Michael do here? Is this where he wrote *Minister without Portfolio*? The house is painted salmon pink with black trim. I wondered how I would animate this sparse landscape enough to hold its own in the portrait, and then I realized I could paint it pink, like the house. Perfect. **/JH**

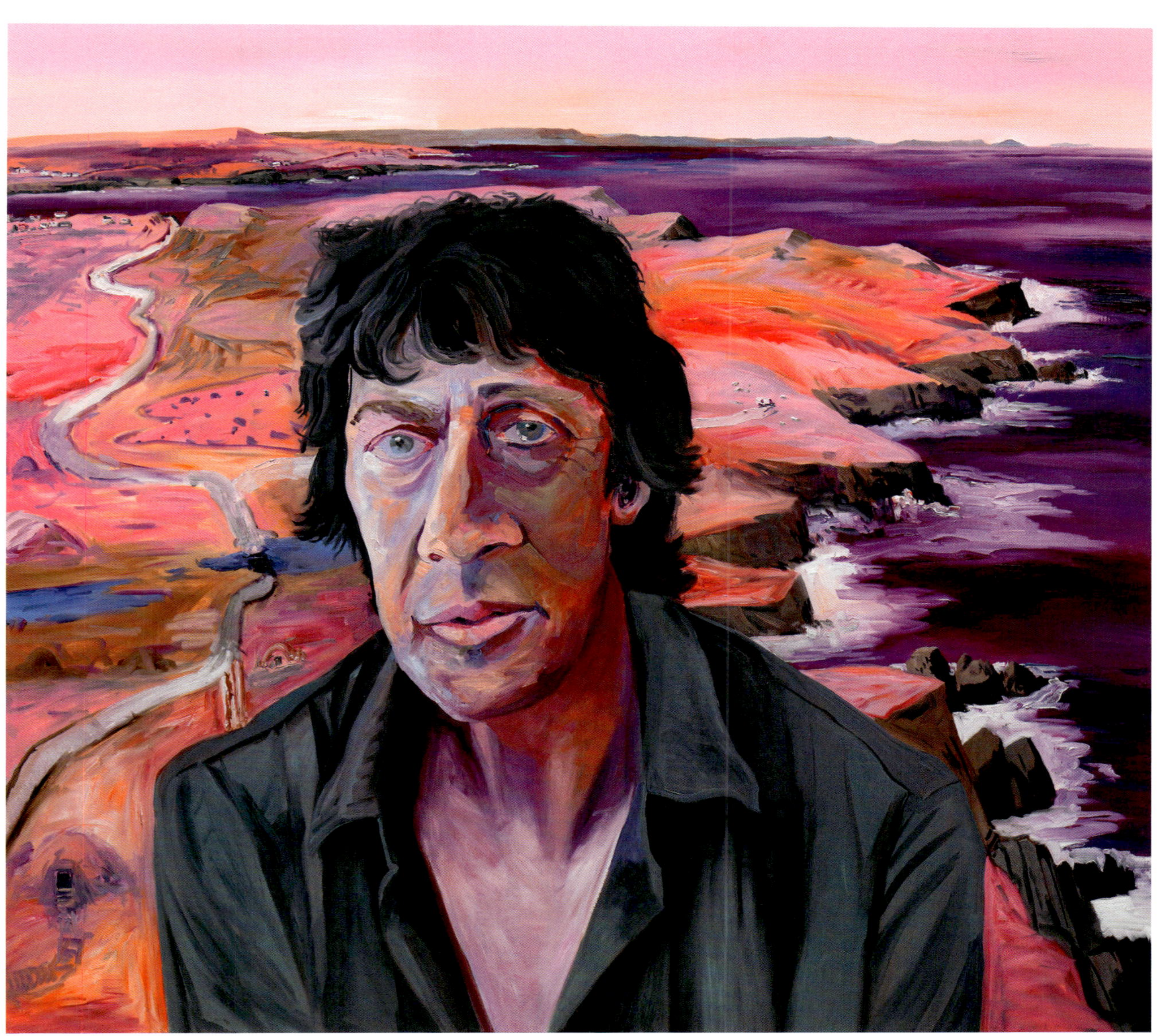

MICHAEL WINTER

Pyramid

IN MY EARLY TWENTIES, I said goodbye to Newfoundland and set off to see the pyramids. An old man asked if I'd take a rock with me. "When you're inside Cheops' tomb," he said, "toss it into a corner near the sarcophagus."

I asked him why.

"It's labradorite," he said. "I want to confuse the archaeologists."

In my thirties, I moved to Toronto but always rented a summer place back in Newfoundland. One morning, in the middle of a bad winter, I got a message from a friend. There's a house for sale around the bay, he said. Was I interested?

I had just won a short story contest, and it was my birthday. The prize money was precisely the cost of the house. I took it as a sign. "I'll fly down."

There is nothing more dispiriting than inspecting a cold, abandoned house with no running water or electricity. I had no family connection here. No history. I knew nothing of this town or its people, and thought I never would. "It's perfect," I thought.

I've spent a dozen summers fixing that house up. At first, I thought it was the closeness to the sea that I loved. But I realized I wasn't looking at the ocean much: it was the land. I loved taking the rough path out to the abandoned community of Bradley's Cove. All that remains are shale foundations. There's a stone cellar, covered in

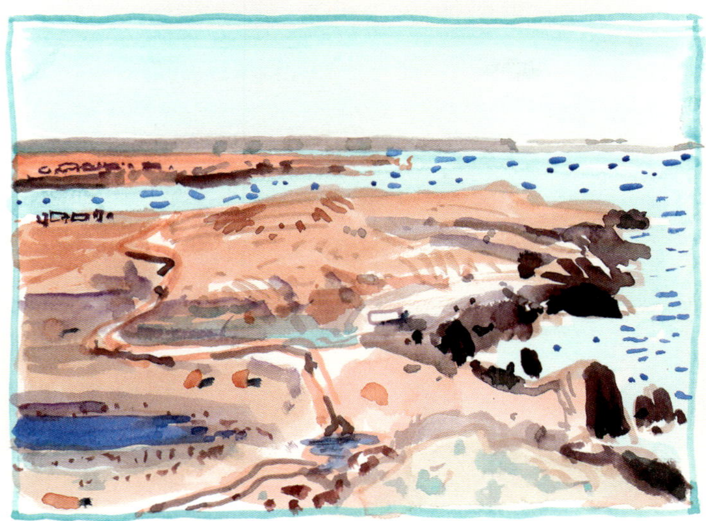

Bradley's Cove 2016
watercolour on paper
9.25" × 11.25"

turf. You can stand in that cellar and, once your eyes have adjusted, peer onto what must have been. It makes you think: of who lived here, and what it looked like crammed with houses and animals and fish stores.

I was digging a well and asked the man who supplied stone for its walls where he got the rock. "From old foundations," he said. "And dismantling cellars."

And then, last summer, a stranger let himself in. I was having my lunch. "I'm looking for the owner of the house," he said. He was old but strong.

"You're looking at him."

He noticed a bowl of bananas on the windowsill.

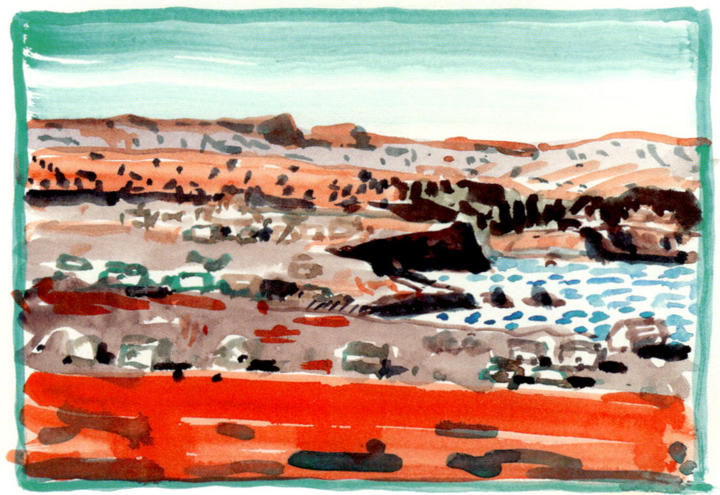

Western Bay 2016
watercolour on paper
9.25″ × 11.25″

"It must be going on eighty years," he said, "when old George Loveys handed me my first banana. I was standing right on this spot."

I knew that George Loveys had built this house in 1906, but that's all I knew of him. I reached over to the bowl and tore off a banana. "It's time for another one," I said.

He was dropping by because he had a memoir written by a relation, and this house is mentioned several times. He thought I might like to look at it.

And then he sat down and told me all about the Loveys family, and the neighbours, and who lived up and down this shore.

The memoir, unpublished, names the brook out back, the hill I stare at, and everyone who lived in Bradley's Cove. It describes the train that used to run and where the boats docked, the location of the blacksmith and the church and school. The man who had written it had left this headland for the Boston States. He'd become a scientist. He worked, if you can believe it, on the Manhattan Project. And George Loveys, the man who had built this house, is quoted in the memoir telling this future scientist, "Go away from here—make your living by the pen."

And I thought, I make my living by the pen.

Recently, I came across some colour slides of life in Bradley's Cove, and saw for the first time the structures that stood upon those shale foundations. Men, women, and children standing outside brightly painted homes. I knew, from figuring out where in the cove the houses were situated and applying facts from the memoir, who these people must be. And walking now into this abandoned cove, I can see them, projected phantoms above these stone footings.

Before I left that summer, I took one last walk into Bradley's Cove. I stood in the cellar. I fear that my well builder will tear it down someday, but for now I'm happy things are staying as they are. I realized I was looking for the anomaly. As a writer you focus on the object that doesn't belong to explain the whole—the labradorite in the tomb of Cheops. And I understood that I was the anomaly. If Western Bay is my Cairo, then Bradley's Cove is its Giza—this cellar, my pyramid. ■

DAVID MACFARLANE ABOVE HAMILTON

2014 | oil on linen, 60″ × 66″

DAVID MACFARLANE'S WAS the first portrait that I painted in this series. In fact, when I made it in 2014, I didn't know that this would become a series. After photographing David in my studio, I asked him what place he would like in his portrait. He said Hamilton, specifically his childhood home and the pool in its backyard. I had just finished reading *The Figures of Beauty*, which had won the F.G. Bressani Literary Prize, so I was aware of the pool and its outsized presence in the neighbourhood. David told me that he had written a good part of the novel in the pool house. But David's mother had recently died, and David and his siblings had sold the property. They were about to clear out the belongings.

We met at the house, walked up to the pool, and continued up the escarpment, known locally as the Mountain. There we had a great view across the city and Hamilton Harbour—almost as far as Toronto. Eventually, I figured out how to combine the pool and its unusual light, the family home, and the view of the neighbourhood from the mountain above.

When I had finished, an unusual thing happened: David asked if I would lend him the painting to install in his living room. He wanted to understand what he was seeing when he looked at it. We installed it, and five years later David has written *Likeness,* a book that interweaves his memories of growing up in Hamilton with his experience of looking at the first portrait of this series. **/JH**

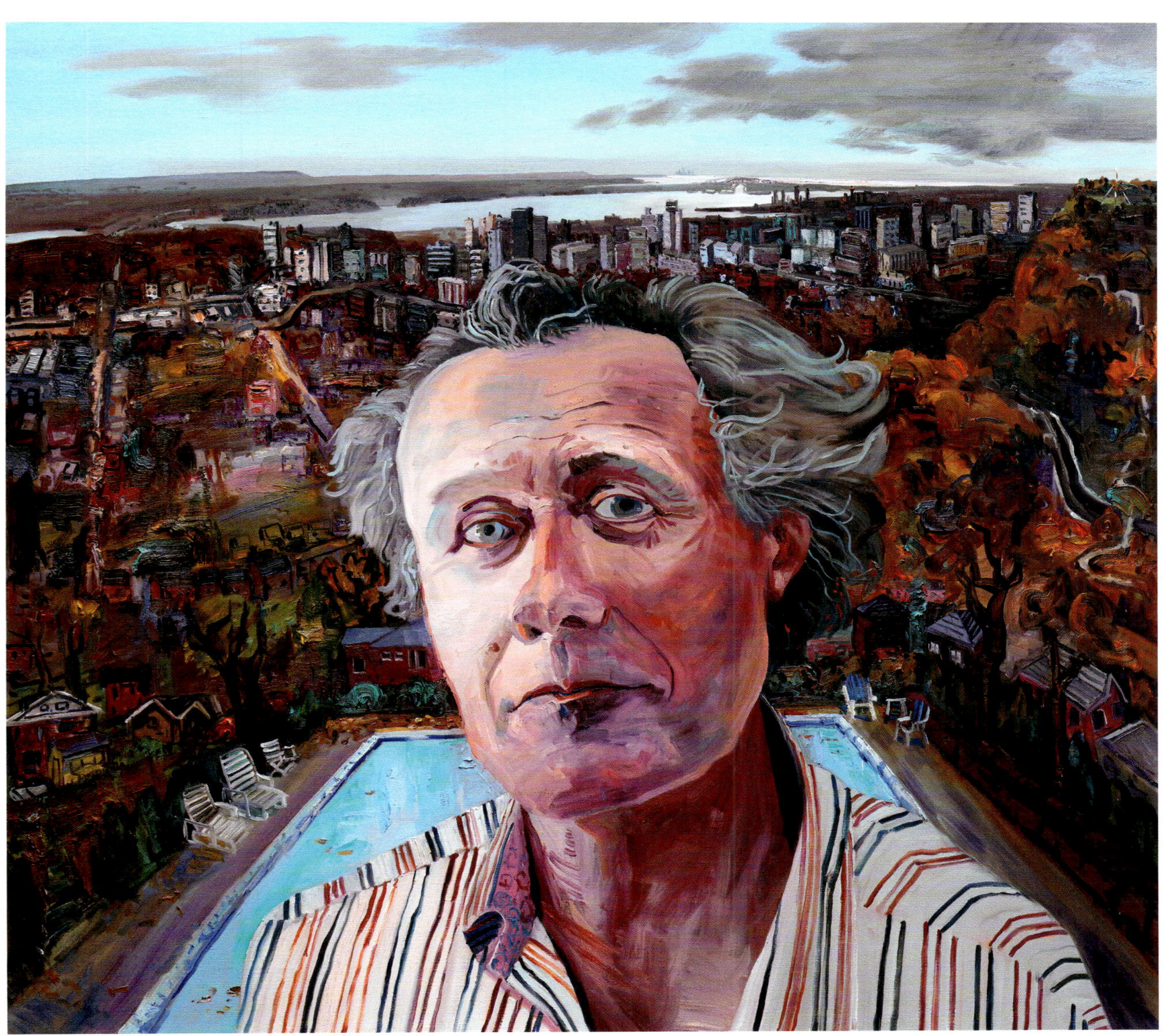

DAVID MACFARLANE

The Pool

NOTHING WILL MORE firmly affix my identification with the middle class than the swimming pool in John Hartman's oil painting. Aptly enough, it's in the middle.

I'm in the foreground of the stretched Belgian linen, sixty by sixty-six inches, that Hartman painted in his studio in the fall of 2014. Hamilton, the city where I grew up, stretches to Lake Ontario in the background. But central to everything is the turquoise rectangle of my parents' pool.

It was built in 1965. That was when I turned thirteen, and I loved it from my first dive. As further evidence of my bourgeois roots, the pool was (and now that the property belongs to someone else, it persists in memory as) one of my favourite places in the world.

My father was frugal. He was an eye doctor, the son of a Hamilton ear, nose, and throat man. So we were comfortable. We were secure. Compared to the vast majority of the earth's population, we were wealthy. But this (I am now embarrassed to admit) was not obvious to me—mostly because my father was so careful about money. Our not-all-that-big house was draughty in winter and, for most of my growing up, not air-conditioned in summer. My hockey shin pads were magazines held in place by elastic bands. My father was past forty before he conceded to a car salesman, finally, and agreed to pay the extra for a radio.

A swimming pool was the last thing we expected. It was entirely out of character for my father. At Burlington Beach and at cottages our family sometimes visited, he demonstrated a remarkable facility for floating on his back. It was as if he had an invisible air mattress. But I'd never seen him dive or take a stroke of front crawl. So far as we knew, he wasn't a pool enthusiast.

But a neighbour had decided to sell the lot behind our backyard, and in order to protect our privacy, my father bought it. I believe the price tag was $1,800. My parents lived (as can be seen in the painting) on the lower slope of the Niagara Escarpment, and our newly acquired lot was a narrow plateau beyond the gloomy cedar hedge at the upper end of their garden. There was an old fire trap of a barn that my father had torn down, and once it was gone, there was pretty much nothing there. Until the pool.

Its dimensions were predicated not by any grandiosity on my father's part, but by the size of the lot. It would have been silly to install a small pool amid so much vacancy. To the surprise of our friends and neighbours, we became the family with a large turquoise rectangle at the back of our garden.

This was just before Expo. Just before Trudeaumania. Just before *Sgt. Pepper* and Woodstock and the first man on the moon. And, for me, the advent of the pool was just before girls, which was pretty much perfect (graduation parties, bikinis). It was all quite miraculous, really. Although the sad truth is: we were so naive in those days, and so rich, we thought miracles, like swimming pools, were just the way things were. ■

HEATHER O'NEILL AT PRINCE ARTHUR AND DE BULLION STREETS

2018 | **oil on linen, 60″ × 66″**

AT THE BEGINNING of Heather O'Neill's 2017 Kreisel Lecture, she tells the story of her early childhood. She was born in Montreal, where she lived until she was five, when her parents divorced. Her mother loaded her into their car and drove to Virginia. They moved around for two and a half years, at which point she told Heather that "she had changed her mind about wanting to be my mother." She put Heather on a plane back to Montreal, where Heather spent the rest of her childhood with her father. "My dad was a petty criminal as a child," she recalls. "He was in prison when he was eleven years old. As an adult, he worked as a janitor." She goes on to describe her father as a caring, if unorthodox, parent. Heather's lecture was published by the University of Alberta Press as *Wisdom in Nonsense: Invaluable Lessons from My Father.*

It's tempting to imagine Heather's fictional characters as versions of her and her father, particularly in her second novel, *The Girl Who Was Saturday Night*, from 2013. Her 2006 debut, *Lullabies for Little Criminals*, was a Canadian and international bestseller, and it won the Paragraphe Hugh MacLennan Prize for Fiction.

Heather hesitated when I asked her where she'd like me to set her painting. When I finally got there, I wanted to check that I had the correct place. She had described a large mural in a square, in Montreal's Plateau district, where she would sit as a child and imagine what the female figures in the mural were doing. I photographed the wall and sent Heather an email. Yes, she said, I had found the right spot. **/JH**

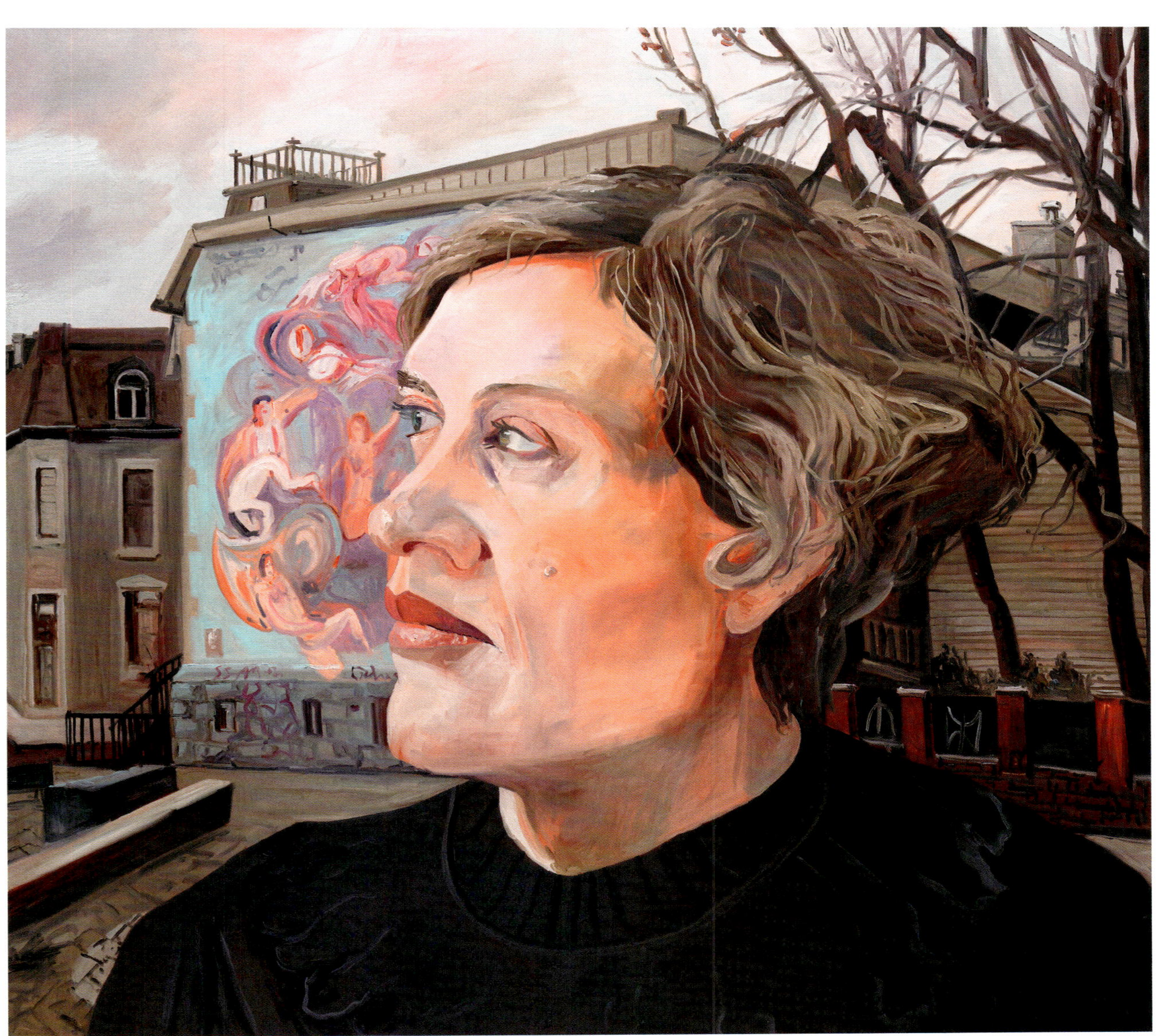

HEATHER O'NEILL

Prince Arthur Street

THIS PAINTING DEPICTS a mural on Prince Arthur Street, which leads up to Saint-Louis Square, in Montreal. Growing up, it was the very heart of the neighbourhood known as the Plateau. The rents were ludicrously cheap, and the area was filled with artists and riff-raff. I spent a good portion of my youth living within a few blocks of this street. And all my happiest childhood memories took place somewhere near, if not on, it. Because of this area, I became hopelessly bohemian and measured every place in the world by the standards set for me here.

The neighbourhood itself has changed. The rents began to go up in the late 1990s, causing a mass exodus of artists toward the northern neighbourhood above Mont Royal, called Mile End. Prince Arthur Street is under interminable construction now. The city decided to make it into something pretty, and that's ruining the economy of every shop on it and has destroyed the makeshift glory of what it once was.

It used to be a wondrous street, always filled with tables outside of the restaurants and street performers on every block. I beheld the most dynamic spectacles right in front of this fountain. People would perch on its side to watch. My father never paid for us to see an actual show inside of a theatre. It wouldn't have occurred to him. But he would bring me here almost every night in the summertime, and we would sit together and take in the productions of dancers, musicians, and magicians. I came to have a deep love of theatre through what I saw each evening, as the sun went down and the street lights came on and people became progressively drunker and more stoned and euphoric.

There were accordion players with singers. Because I was a child, they did not seem to be amateurish whatsoever. Their songs were deeply moving, and the trumpet playing was that of angels. There were oddball songsters in suits with microphones attached to small amplifiers who were as romantic and poetic as Leonard Cohen. My favourite was when there were clowns and actors. There was one clown who opened an umbrella and small paper snowflakes blew all over his head. This obvious Brechtian trick had an impact on the way I write metaphors. The puppet shows made me believe that you could fit the meaning of life into a trunk and pull it out on a street corner and express it to wide-eyed children.

I still feel so filled with delight when I pass this mural. I remember letting go of my father's hand and pressing to the front of a crowd to sit cross-legged on my sweater on the ground and watch a woman in black hair dance a wild modern-dance number while a man played an electric piano for her and laughed. ■

IAN BROWN
ABOVE GO HOME BAY

2017 | **oil on linen, 60″ × 66″**

IAN BROWN IS a journalist, author, and radio and TV host. He has published four books and is best known for *The Boy in the Moon: A Father's Search for His Disabled Son*. In 2010, it won the British Columbia National Award for Canadian Non-Fiction, as well as the Charles Taylor Prize.

Ian told me there was a point of land, on an island on the outside edge of Go Home Bay, in Georgian Bay, that he would like in his portrait. It was not his: it was a friend's cottage property that Ian and his wife, Johanna, and their two children used to rent. He said that it provided a spectacular view to the open water of Georgian Bay, across to the Pine Islands and out as far as Christian and Hope Islands. This was very much the view that Frederick Varley painted in his iconic masterpiece, *Stormy Weather, Georgian Bay*. Ian said that the broad and smooth open rock at the front of the island was a perfect place to paint watercolours, and then to jump into the water if the summer heat was too much.

I sketched and photographed the island in late November, in a bit of a rush, not long before the ice formed. But I painted as if it were summer. **/JH**

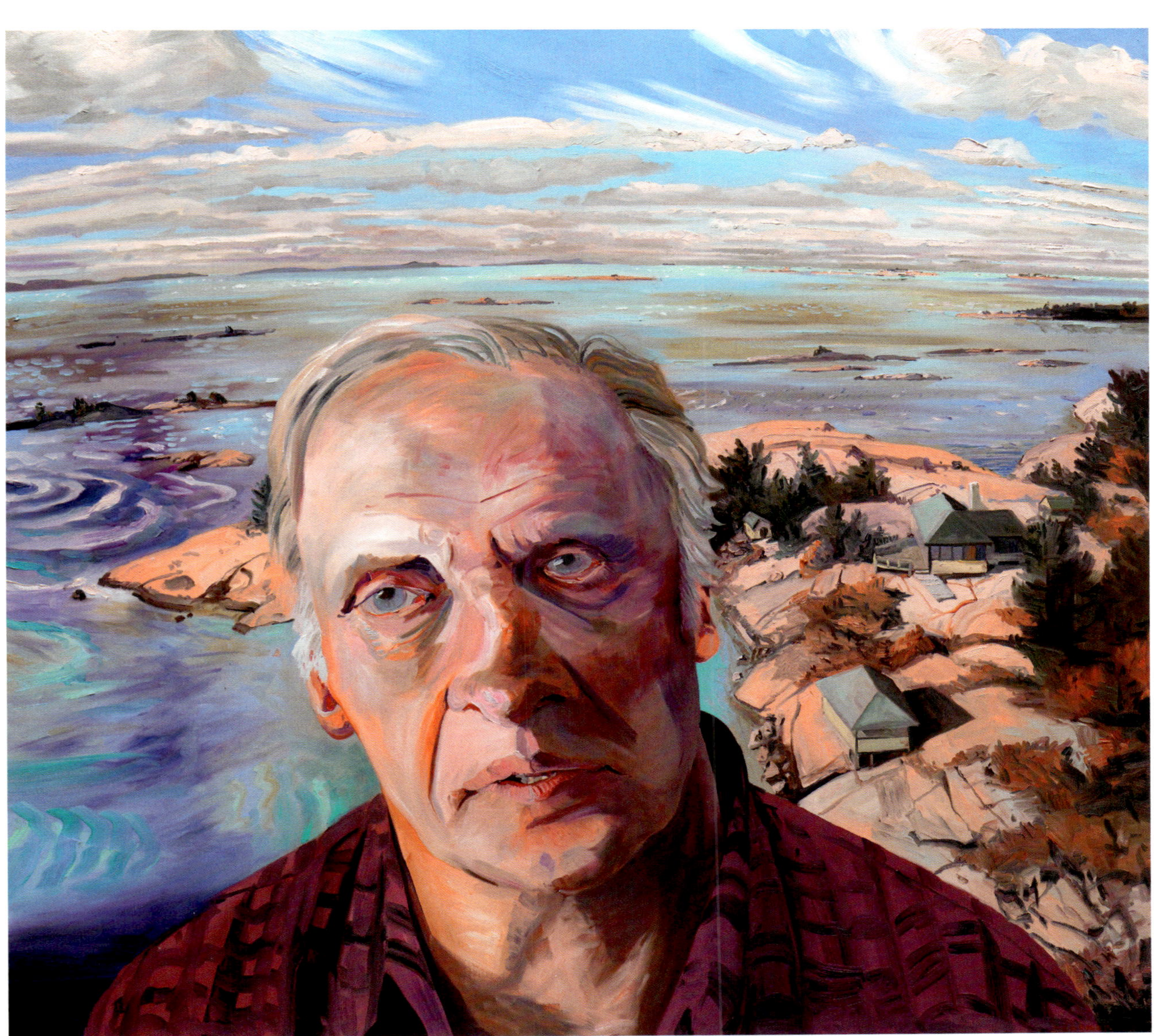

IAN BROWN

That Place

THE WHITE COTTAGE at the mouth of Go Home Bay was the first summer place I ever rented on Georgian Bay. I was in my early forties, the breaking point in a man's life, and the cottage satisfied several requirements: it was spare, beautiful, and on a lively and changeable body of water. The bay reminded me of the Atlantic shore on Cape Ann, north of Boston, where I grew up with my brothers and sisters. It was also secluded: the only way to get to the cottage was a two-and-a-half-hour drive followed by a serious forty-minute boat ride over open water. My wife and I had a young family and felt like we had found our place, a place just for us and for anyone who wanted to be with us.

While it was remote, and far away from doctors, which we, strictly speaking, ought to have been closer to, especially after Walker came along—he had been born disabled with a shockingly rare genetic syndrome that had turned our lives inside out—it was also a place where Walker could be who he was, free from the stares and expectations of others. As could the rest of us. The light and the wind seemed to change my son, calm him down, and also inspire my daughter. Hayley made bead curtains and read to herself and to us, and she learned to swim. (I have a picture of that moment in my bedroom. It's my favourite of all I own: Hayley standing to her waist in the water, hands on her hips, her elation expanding as she realizes what she has just accomplished. My wife says it is an image she wants to keep in her mind when it is her time to leave the world.) Hayley and I also did a lot of painting, if you could call it that, out on the flat granite Canadian Shield slabs that tumble down from the white cottage to the water. We'd sit on the point with our watercolours, with Walker in his travelling crib, and we'd sketch and swim, sketch and swim. It makes me cry to remember it—not because that time is gone but because we experienced its astonishing peace and privacy and pleasure together, full of hope.

It was also the last place we vacationed before I took on a brace of full-time jobs at the CBC and the *Globe and Mail* to make more money, before the world consumed us. In 1998, the first summer we rented the cottage, Hayley was five and Walker was two. That was the year a developmental pediatrician revealed how delayed Walker actually was. He told us Walker would never read or drive a car. Then he asked if I had any questions. I replied by explaining how Walker changed when we went up to the island, how he seemed to lift his head toward the light and the breeze in the west, and settle. I asked if I would ever be able to explain to Walker how much that place meant to me.

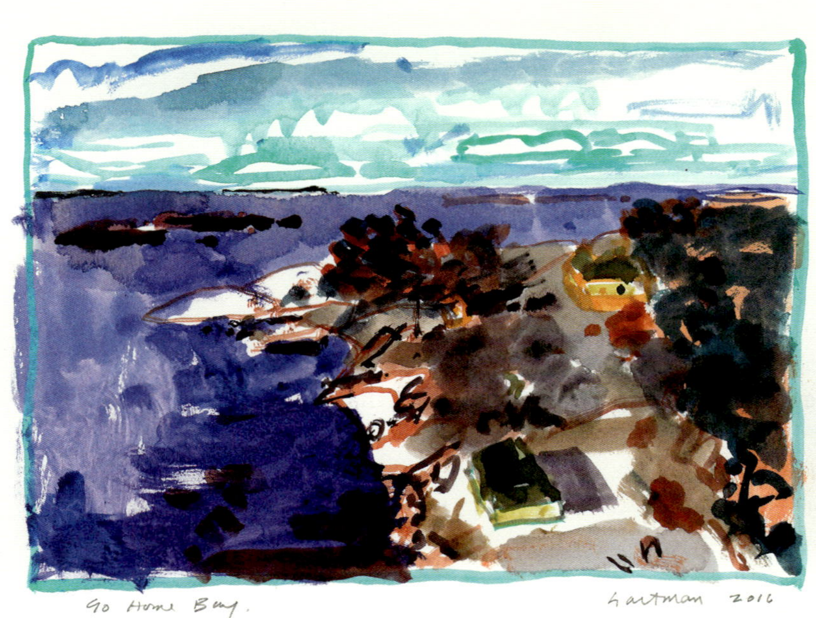

Go Home Bay 2016
watercolour on paper
9.25″ × 11.25″

"Not rationally, no," the doctor replied. "But it sounds as if he already understands it anyway, in his being. You know what the Buddhists say: get out of the way of your own mind. In that way, Walker's miles ahead of all of us."

It was also at the white cottage on the island, amid all that beauty and nature and stillness, that Hayley and I first forged our relationship, our closeness. Because of her, I think of the island and the cottage and the sleeping cabins and the water and the bent trees and the rocks—all of it—as this incredibly deep and meaningful place, full of all the grace of the world. Everything was an adventure: the blueberry picking, the possibility of snakes, the bears, the slithery cold of the water. I could think about all that forever. It still calms me down when I do. ■

CHIC SCOTT ABOVE PEYTO LAKE AND THE PEYTO GLACIER

2017 | **oil on linen, 68″ × 48″**

CHIC SCOTT IS one of Canada's leading mountaineers and a literary authority on the history of the Rockies. He has turned the life experiences of his climbing contemporaries into an important record by capturing them in prose.

I could have painted him in almost any place along the Great Divide, or as far west as the Monashee Mountains, but Chic was quick to say that he wanted to be painted on the Peyto Glacier, where it becomes part of the Wapta Icefield. This was the first icefield he experienced, in 1964 at age nineteen. I have watched Chic move gracefully through this landscape, as only someone who has spent a lifetime paying attention to it can.

Chic and I drove to Peyto Lake from Banff one glorious morning in late April. I needed some photos, so we stopped by the side of the road, close to the point where a backcountry skier might set out to cross the lake and ascend the glacier. It was cloudy, but the weather was moving fast from the west. Chic walked down the road for a better view of the incoming weather, watched for about ten minutes, then came back to the car and told me, correctly, that in twenty minutes a clear section between the clouds would pass over, casting sunlight onto the lake and the glacier, and giving me the perfect moment to take my photographs. **/JH**

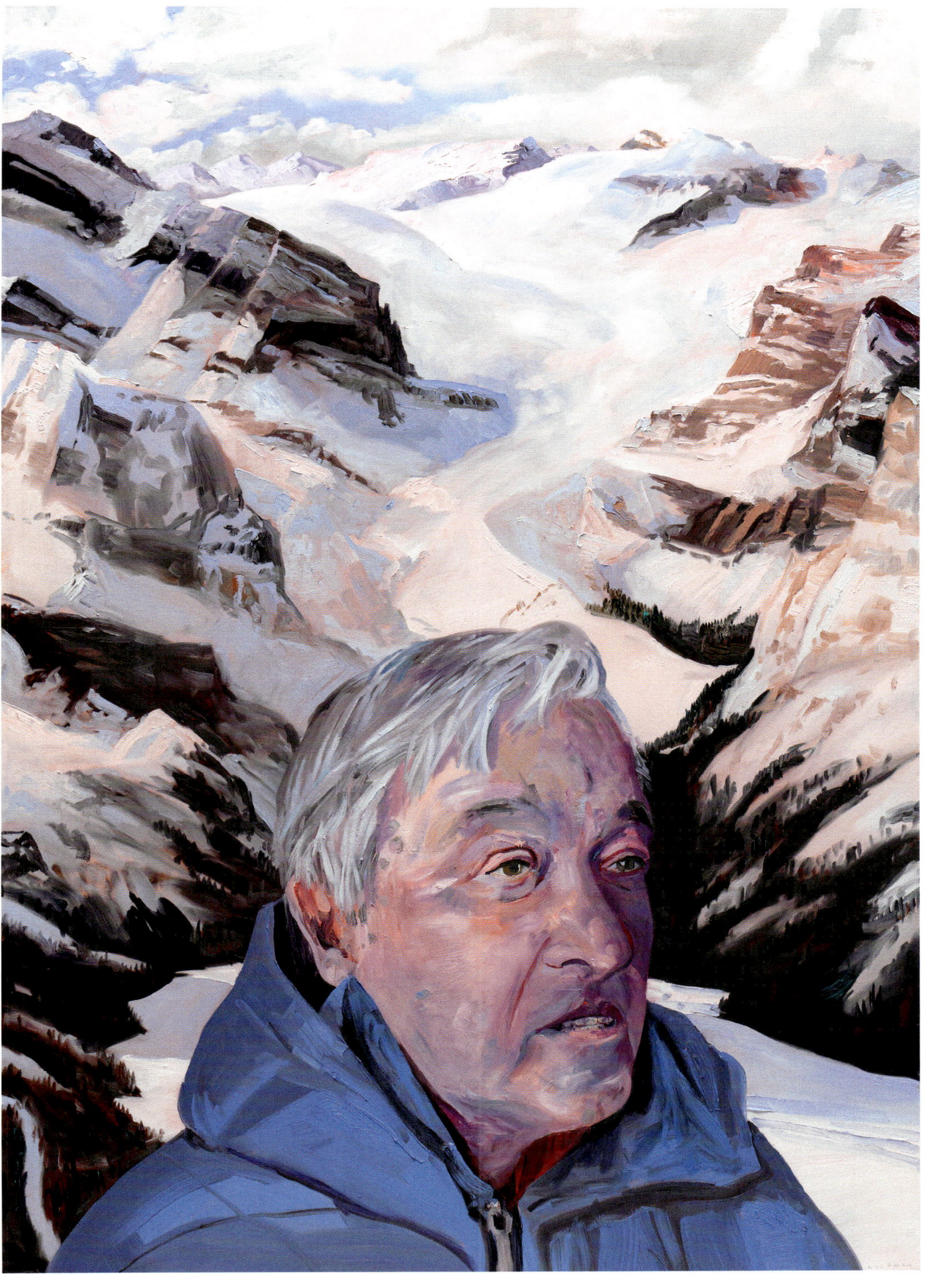

CHIC SCOTT

An Alpine World

WHEN I DISCOVERED the Rocky Mountains as a teenager, it was as if a door opened from the box that I had been living in and I stepped into a magic world of peaks and stars, the smell of wood smoke and the soughing of the wind in the pines. It was springtime: the sap was rising in the trees, and the melting snow was dripping off the roof of our wilderness cabin. I fell in love with the mountains, and for almost sixty years now my life has been devoted to the great ranges of the world.

The first icefield that I ventured onto was the Wapta Icefield, northwest of Lake Louise. My best friend, Gerry Walsh, and I skied from the Icefields Parkway across Peyto Lake, up a canyon and onto the Peyto Glacier. Late in the afternoon, we set up our tent, my first night camped on a glacier. It was a cold and alien world, but so pure and beautiful. This was 1964, and there were no huts and very few ski mountaineers in the area. It was our private alpine paradise for a few days, our sacred country.

Since then I have spent many hundreds of nights camped in the snow, on glaciers and icefields. I have skied ten grand traverses across the immense glacial wilderness of Western Canada. I have carefully threaded crevasses and negotiated steep avalanche slopes. In cloud and fog, I have made my way forward with compass in hand. At night I have lain in my sleeping bag and listened to the snow, blown by the wind, brush against the tent walls. In morning light, shovel in hand, I have dug our little shelter from the drifts. Then, back in the tent, I have sat contentedly and made tea and listened to the stove purr. In other words, in a white and frozen world, I have found a home and made a beautiful peace with myself.

The high alpine world is an intellectual place, one of philosophy and contemplation. Unlike the oceans and jungles, there is little life, little distraction. There are few sounds: The wind, of course, always the wind. The occasional crack from the ice or the rumble of a distant avalanche. Rarely, a raven flies over and says hello with a raucous cry.

As I grow older, it becomes harder for me to venture into this world. My bones ache sleeping on a thin pad, and the cold penetrates even the most modern down clothing. But I have my photographs, and I have my memories. I have been there. I have known the perfection of wind-blown snow. I have known the relentless roar of the blizzard. And I have known the infinite beauty of the starlit sky. Orion is an old friend.

I will ski my last icefield sometime soon, but it will not be a sad moment. It will be a time to rejoice at the great blessing of a rich and adventurous life. ■

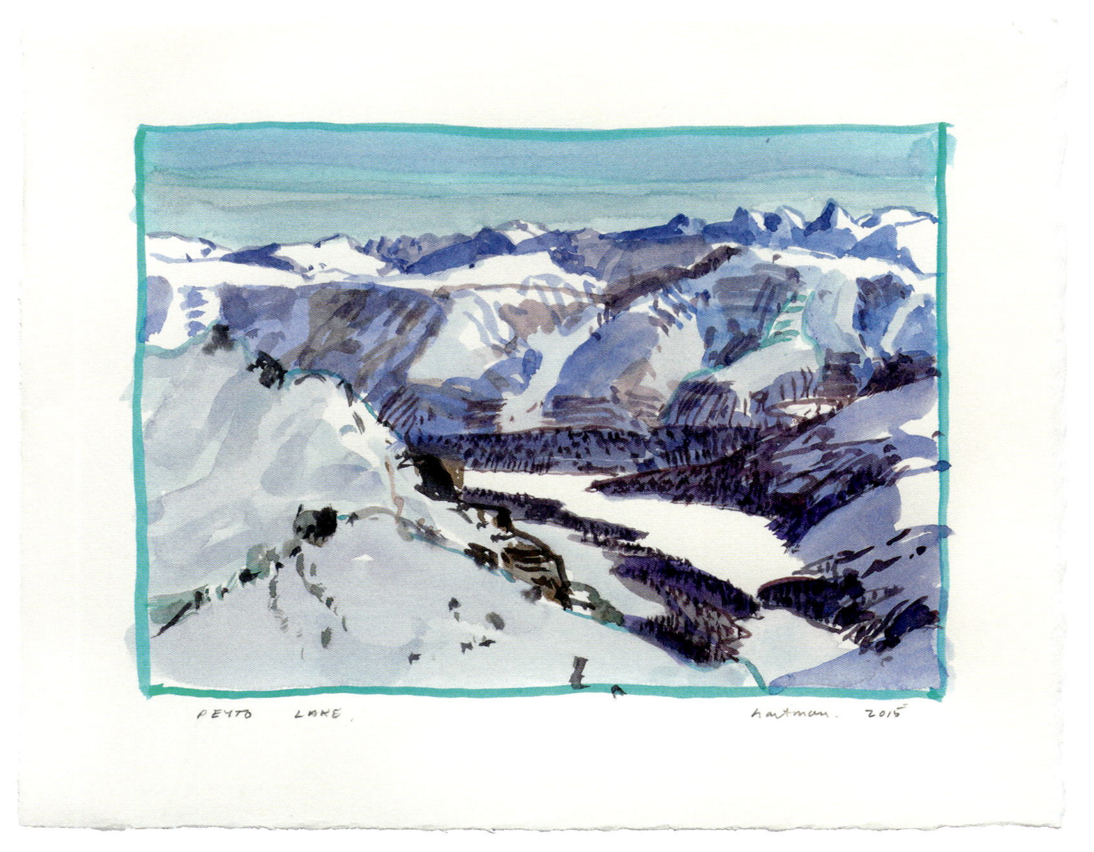

Peyto Lake 2015
watercolour on paper
9″ × 11.5″

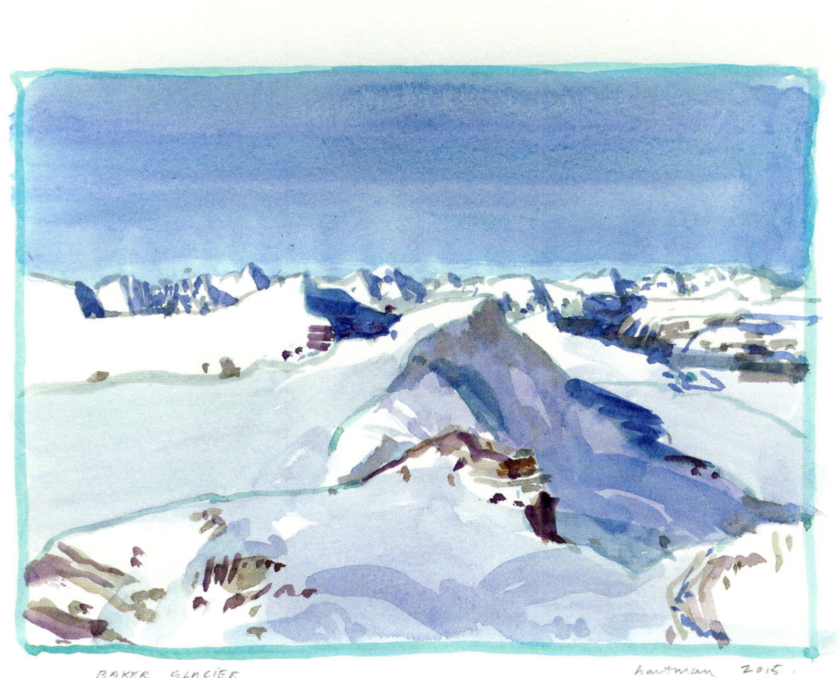

Baker Glacier 2015
watercolour on paper
9″ × 11″

MARY LYNK
ABOVE GREEN BAY

2018 | **oil on linen, 48″ × 54″**

IN THE UPPER left corner of this painting, on the last point of land, you can see Blueberry Hill Cottage, where Mary Lynk was conceived. Following the shoreline to the lower right corner, you see two enormous beach boulders. Mary told me her late aunt and a suitor were thought to meet there furtively at night. You can still see their names, carved into the rock in the 1940s. Mary made a point of showing me both of these places on the tour she gave me of the Green Bay shoreline.

Mary and her partner, Sandy Graham, had recently purchased a home in West Dublin, down the road from Green Bay, and Mary was clearly excited to show me spots she had known since childhood. Places that resonated with her mother's family history.

Mary is a producer and documentary maker with CBC Radio's *Ideas,* and when I listen to her stories on air, I am always taken with the curiosity, care, and daring with which she approaches each subject. If something has caught her attention, she wants to know why, and she will pursue the answer until she does. Then she tells us the story. **/JH**

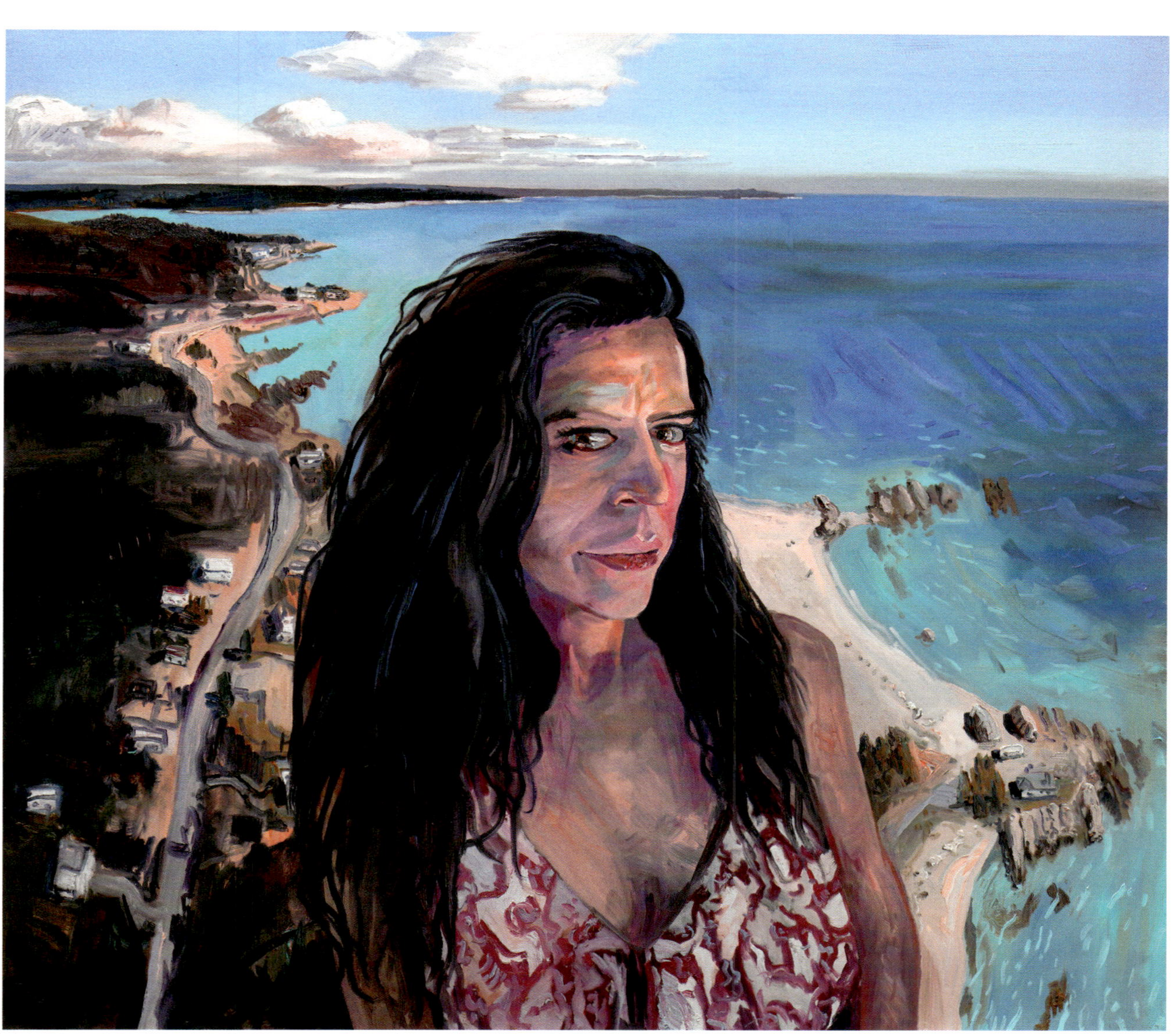

MARY LYNK

Uncle Neiff

A FEW MOMENTS AGO, on a September day disguised in warmth and perfection as midsummer, I put my hand in a plastic zip-lock bag and grabbed a fistful of ashes, human ashes.

To be more precise, I grabbed bits and pieces of my beloved Uncle Neiff.

At first I was going to use rubber gloves. But then I remembered a few months ago, holding his hand at the hospital down the road in Bridgewater—the small town where he was born, grew up, and died at eighty-one.

He was the youngest child of immigrants from Bakka, Syria, and later, because of the Balfour Declaration's disregard of boundaries, Bakka, Lebanon. His father, my grandfather, Mahfoath—Charlie to the locals—was a peddler travelling up and down the coastal road seen in the painting. Selling everything—cloth to flour to nails—from his horse-drawn wagon.

My family is carved deep into this landscape. So it felt wrong not to hold my uncle again, with my bare hands. Even if the texture is no longer soft Arab skin, but a mixture of fine, gritty sand.

No matter, it's still Uncle Neiff.

Death is death. Not to be afraid of—not to shy away from.

Now look at the painting again. To the right, by the lower part of my arm, there's a large rock on a white sandy beach. That's where

I just was, reaching into the bag: Green Bay, where about seventy years ago, my mother's sister (and most likely my uncle's favourite sister), Audrey, had her name carved into that rock.

Her lover's name, perhaps, carved on top.

Where maybe, or at least according to a *New Yorker* short story by my cousin Rick Rofihe, my Uncle Neiff buried some, if not all, of Audrey's ashes in the late 1960s:

> A hundred miles inland, where you didn't take me, where the stone with her full name and full years are, and where you finally had to let it go, what's buried there? What's in the jar? A fifty-fifty mix? Sand and ashes? Or is she, all of her, outside and inside, at the base of that rock near the beach? . . . Where I saw you—I saw you!—dig your hands deep into warm sand.

I wonder, just now, if the kid playing Frisbee with his dog saw me, kneeling before that same rock, bury a handful of Uncle Neiff's ashes into the sand.

My uncle stopped believing in God after Audrey's death in her early thirties from Crohn's disease. He told me this as he lay dying. How angry he was then. How he wasn't afraid to die now, not believing.

At the rock, I ran my hand over the deep grooves that clearly spell *Audrey*.

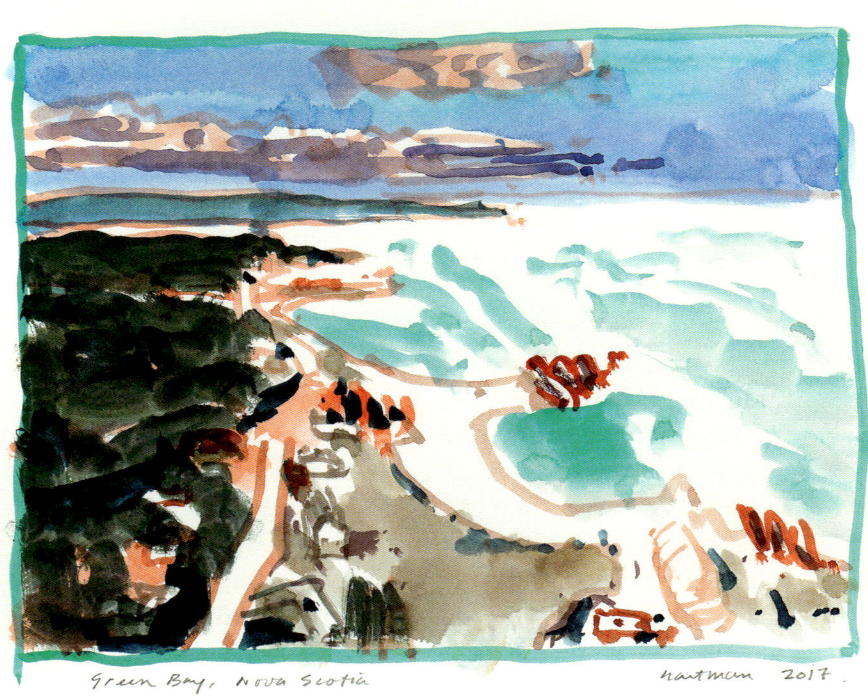

Green Bay, Nova Scotia 2017
watercolour on paper
9.25″ × 11.25″

The sea has worn out much of the lover's name on top.

The carving took place when she was young. He was likely Christian, and her Muslim parents unaware.

My grandparents were aware of not belonging to the community, yet of belonging to the land. In the painting, just up from the rock, is a seaside cottage—called Blueberry Hill—where my late mother, Sarah, said I was conceived.

You can still rent that cottage from the MacLeod family. The dividing walls remain a challenge to anyone trying to make love with two young sons sleeping next door.

And just past that, up the shoreline, is the summer home we recently bought—my husband, daughter, and I.

Because the pull of the place where you find refuge, peddle your wares, are conceived, your mother is born, your aunt falls in love, your uncle dies, and ashes are slyly buried—the pull never lets go.

Bakka is still Bakka, no matter if it's in Syria or Lebanon.

It stirs my family regardless of boundaries, as does this shoreline.

Land where important things happen deeply engraves us. A rock that pulls us back. Ashes to sand. ■

Acknowledgements

IN THE BEGINNING, a project like this is just an idea. As such it requires faith on the part of those who support it. I want to thank Nicholas Metivier of the Nicholas Metivier Gallery in Toronto, Christina Parker of the Christina Parker Gallery in St. John's, and Mary Reid, the director of the Woodstock Art Gallery, for their unwavering early support. John Macfarlane's contribution as editor and adviser has been immense. At John's side doing the copy edit and fact checking was Kyle Wyatt. David Macfarlane's was the first portrait I painted in this series. He had many roles and has always been at hand to give advice when asked, which was frequently. Sarah Milroy, chief curator at the McMichael Canadian Art Collection, has been a constant help.

Thanks to the curators of the Bonavista Biennale, Pat Grattan and Catherine Beaudette, for including four of these portraits in the inaugural Biennale in 2017.

I have always benefitted from my family's support and this project was no exception. To Trish, Catherine, Marie, David, and Joseph, thank you. In addition, Joseph Hartman photographed the finished portraits and prepared the digital files. David Hartman documented much of the studio work on film.

As this project neared completion, many details needed attention. Sarah Massie and Caroline Pearson at the Nicholas Metivier Gallery were a great help.

The team at Figure 1 Publishing—Chris Labonté, Mike Leyne, Jessica Sullivan, Lara Smith, Michelle Meade, and Mark Redmayne—have been a joy to work with.

Each author took a risk when they said yes, not knowing what their final portrait would look like. For your dedicated participation and wonderful essays, I thank each of you.

JOHN HARTMAN, RCA

JOHN HARTMAN was born in 1950 in Midland, Ontario. He first earned a reputation for his inventive, large-scale landscapes with the exhibition *Painting the Bay* (1993). He gained national and international attention with *Big North* (an exhibition that toured Canada from 1999 to 2002) and *Cities* (which toured Canada and overseas from 2007 to 2009). He lives in Lafontaine, Ontario.

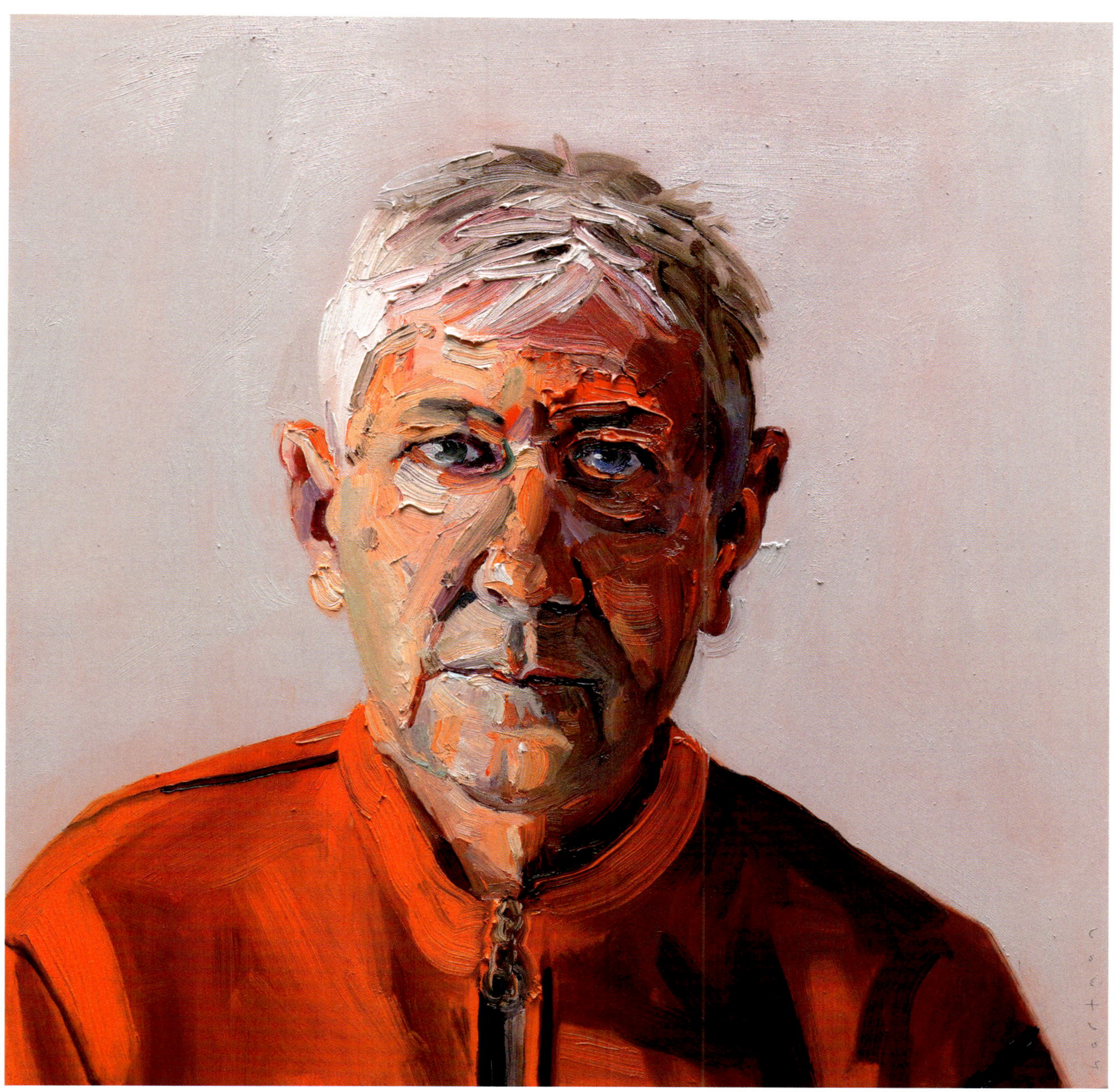

Self-Portrait 2019
oil on panel
16″ × 16″

SELECTED SOLO EXHIBITIONS

2020-2022
Many Lives Mark This Place, curated by Mary Reid, Woodstock Art Gallery, Woodstock, ON. Travelling to McMichael Canadian Art Collection, Kleinburg, ON, 2020; Audain Art Museum, Whistler, 2020–2021; Judith & Norman Alix Art Gallery, Sarnia, ON, 2021; Confederation Art Centre Gallery, Charlottetown, 2021; Woodstock Art Gallery, Woodstock, ON, 2022

2018, 2016, 2014, 2010-2012, 2008, 2007, 2005
Nicholas Metivier Gallery, Toronto

2017
Across the Great Divide: Paintings by John Hartman, Whyte Museum of the Canadian Rockies, Banff

2017, 2013, 2009
Christina Parker Gallery, St. John's

2016, 2013
Arthur Roger Gallery, New Orleans

2015, 2012, 2005-2008, 2003, 2000, 1998
Paul Kuhn Gallery, Calgary

2012
The Columbia River in Canada, curated by Liz Wylie, Kelowna Art Gallery

Shore Line Over View, curated by Jennifer Withrow and Ben Portis, MacLaren Art Centre, Barrie, ON

2007-2009
Cities, curated by Stuart Reid, Tom Thomson Art Gallery, Owen Sound, ON. Travelled to Art Gallery of Calgary, 2007; Art Gallery of Nova Scotia, Halifax (co-organizer), 2007; Southern Alberta Art Gallery, Lethbridge, 2007; Winnipeg Art Gallery, 2007; Art Gallery of Sudbury, 2008; Kenderdine Art Gallery, Saskatoon, 2008; MacLaren Art Centre, Barrie, ON, 2008; University of Toronto Art Centre, 2008; Grenfell Art Gallery, Corner Brook, NL, 2009; The Rooms, St. John's, 2009

2007
Cities, Charles Cowles Gallery, New York

Cities, Jill George Gallery, London, UK

2005
John Hartman: Paintings, Watercolours and Prints of London, Scotland and Canada, Jill George Gallery, London, UK

2004, 2001, 1997–1999, 1995, 1993, 1991, 1990
Mira Godard Gallery, Toronto

1999
Big North, curated by Brian Meehan, Tom Thomson Art Gallery, Owen Sound, ON (co-organizer), and London Regional Art and Historical Museums, London, ON (co-organizer; travelled nationally)

1999, 1997, 1995
Hart Gallery, London, UK

1998
Stories from the Northland, University of Lethbridge Art Gallery

1995
With Minimal Means: John Hartman Prints 1985–1995, curated by Kim Ness, McMaster Museum of Art, Hamilton (travelled nationally)

1993
Painting the Bay: Recent Work by John Hartman, McMichael Canadian Art Collection, Kleinburg, ON

1992
Fired Light—The Glass Paintings of John Hartman from the Workshop of Lars Frese, Copenhagen, London Regional Art and Historical Museums, London, ON (travelled to MacLaren Art Centre, Barrie, ON)

1991
Expulsion from Paradise, an Allegory, 49th Parallel, New York

1988
Invisible Stories, curated by Kim Moodie, Embassy Cultural House, London, ON *The North: Life on the Edge*, curated by Dorothy Farr, Agnes Etherington Art Centre, Kingston, ON

1983
John Hartman—New Paintings and Drawings, curated by Glenn Cumming, Art Gallery of Hamilton

1979–1988
Gadatsy Gallery, Toronto

SELECTED GROUP EXHIBITIONS

2018
Blue Rocks: Gerald Ferguson, Marsden Hartley, and John Hartman, Art Gallery of Nova Scotia, Halifax

2017
Pride of Place: The Making of Contemporary Art in New Orleans, New Orleans Museum of Art, New Orleans

Stone and Sky: Canada's Mountain Landscape, curated by Darrin Martens, Audain Art Museum, Whistler

Bonavista Biennale, curated by Catherine Beaudette and Patricia Grattan, Bonavista Peninsula, NL

2016
Living, Building, Thinking, curated by Ihor Holubizky, McMaster Museum of Art, Hamilton

2014
Changing Tides: Contemporary Art of Newfoundland and Labrador, McMichael Canadian Art Collection, Kleinburg, ON

Land Reform[ed], curated by Stanzie Tooth, Âjagemô, Ottawa

2013
Natural Selection: An Evolving Idea of Canadian Landscape, The Rooms, St. John's

2012
Aspects of a New Kind of Realism, curated by Michael Klein, Arthur Roger Gallery, New Orleans

2008
Invention and Revival: The Colour Drypoints of David Milne and John Hartman, Carleton University Art Gallery, Ottawa. Travelled to the Burnaby Art Gallery, Burnaby, BC

2006
David Alexander and John Hartman, Far and Wide: Alberta Landscapes, Art Gallery of Alberta, Edmonton

1996–1997
Rediscovering the Landscape of the Americas, curated by Alan Gussow, Gerald Peters Gallery, Santa Fe, travelled to Art Museum of South Texas, Corpus Christi, TX, 1997; Gibbes Museum of Art, Charleston, SC, 1997; Memorial Art Gallery, Rochester, NY, 1997; Western Gallery, Bellingham, WA, 1997

1990
Notes from Eden, Tom Thomson Art Gallery, Owen Sound, ON

1989
Glaskunst og Billede, Holstebro Kunstmuseum, Holstebro, Denmark

SELECTED PUBLIC COLLECTIONS

- Agnes Etherington Art Centre, Kingston
- Art Gallery of Alberta, Edmonton
- Art Gallery of Algoma, Sault Ste. Marie, ON
- Art Gallery of Guelph
- Art Gallery of Hamilton
- Art Gallery of Nova Scotia, Halifax
- Art Gallery of Ontario, Toronto
- Art Gallery of Windsor
- Art Museum at the University of Toronto
- Beaverbrook Art Gallery, Fredericton
- British Museum, London, UK
- Canada Council Art Bank, Ottawa
- Carleton University Art Gallery, Ottawa
- Glenbow Museum, Calgary
- Government of Ontario Art Collection, Toronto
- Hart House, Toronto
- Kelowna Art Gallery
- McMaster Museum of Art, Hamilton
- McMichael Canadian Art Collection, Kleinburg, ON
- Masterworks Museum of Bermuda Art
- Museum London, London, ON
- New Orleans Museum of Art
- Remai Modern, Saskatoon
- Robert McLaughlin Gallery, Oshawa, ON
- The Rooms, St. John's
- Royal Library, Copenhagen, Denmark
- Thunder Bay Art Gallery
- Tom Thomson Art Gallery, Owen Sound, ON
- University of Lethbridge Art Gallery
- Winnipeg Art Gallery
- Whyte Museum of the Canadian Rockies, Banff

19 20 21 22 23 5 4 3 2 1

Cataloguing data are available from Library and Archives Canada
ISBN 978-1-77327-094-4 (hbk.)

Design by Jessica Sullivan
Photography by Joseph Hartman
Artworks courtesy of the Nicholas Metivier Gallery, Toronto, except *Esi Edugyan, Victoria*, private collection; *Hamilton Harbour from Upper James St.* and *Hamilton Harbour from Gage St.*, courtesy of McMaster Museum of Art, McMaster University, Hamilton, ON, gifts of the artist, 2010; *Peyto Lake* and *David Adams Richards above the Bartibog and Miramachi Rivers*, collection of Andrew and Valerie Pringle; and *Montreal Harbour*, collection of Sun Life.

Editing by John Macfarlane
Project editing by Michael Leyne
Copy editing by Kyle Wyatt
Proofreading by Michelle Meade

Cover image: *Sara Tilley, Elliston* (detail), 2017.

Printed and bound in Canada by Friesens
Distributed internationally by Publishers Group West

Figure 1 Publishing Inc.
Vancouver BC Canada
figure1publishing.com

Nicholas Metivier Gallery
Toronto ON Canada
metiviergallery.com

Woodstock Art Gallery
Woodstock ON Canada
woodstockartgallery.ca

MANY LIVES MARK THIS PLACE

February to June 2020
McMichael Canadian Art Collection
KLEINBURG, ON

November 2020 to February 2021
Audain Art Museum
WHISTLER, BC

June to September 2021
Judith & Norman Alix Art Gallery
SARNIA, ON

Fall 2021
Confederation Centre Art Gallery
CHARLOTTETOWN, PE

February to June 2022
Woodstock Art Gallery
WOODSTOCK, ON